AWAKE WHERE YOU ARE

AWAKE WHERE YOU ARE

The Art of Embodied Awareness

Martin Aylward

Wisdom

Wisdom Publications
199 Elm Street
Somerville, MA 02144 USA
wisdomexperience.org

Library of Congress Cataloging-in-Publication Data
Names: Aylward, Martin, author.
Title: Awake where you are: the art of embodied awareness / Martin Aylward.
Description: First wisdom edition. | Somerville, MA, USA: Wisdom Publications, 2021. | Includes index.
Identifiers: LCCN 2021005229 (print) | LCCN 2021005230 (ebook) | ISBN 9781614297222 | ISBN 9781614298045 (ebook)
Subjects: LCSH: Meditation. | Awareness | Mindfulness (Psychology) | Contemplation. | Buddhism.
Classification: LCC BL627 .A98 2021 (print) | LCC BL627 (ebook) | DDC 294.3/4435—dc23
LC record available at https://lccn.loc.gov/2021005229
LC ebook record available at https://lccn.loc.gov/2021005230

ISBN 978-1-61429-722-2   ebook ISBN 978-1-61429-804-5

25 24 23 22 21
5 4 3 2 1

Cover design by Phil Pascuzzo. Interior design by Tim Holtz.

Please visit fscus.org.

Contents

Acknowledgments

Whatever teachings and practices I have absorbed over the last thirty years have come been through the kindness and wisdom and blessing of my teachers. My deep gratitude stretches out to them all, but particularly my formal teachers: Ajahn Buddhadasa, Christopher Titmuss, Sukhanta Giri Babaji, Sandra Maitri.

Thank you to Bhikkhu Bodhi, who kindly discussed some Pali translations, and to other writer friends for good advice about the mysterious and challenging art of writing: Stephen Batchelor, Cassandra Pybus, Mark Coleman, Jaya Aylward.

Thank you to all those who have brought this book to life. Especially Catherine Meyer, my endlessly generous and encouraging editor, who showed great faith in my writing without any supporting evidence; Josh Bartok, for laying things out clearly and advocating on my behalf; the team at Wisdom for their patience and indulgence.

And to my family. All of them, but especially to Gail, my wife, whose great support, for my teaching activities and my life in general, has so many dimensions.

Introduction

A Journey to Inner Space

―――――――――――――◆――――――――――

Slow down, you move too fast
You got to make the morning last

—SIMON AND GARFUNKEL, "The 59th Street Bridge
Song (Feelin' Groovy)"

In the thirty years since I sat my first meditation retreat, beginning the journey of contemplative practice that has defined my whole adult life, I've seen the interest in meditation flourish and grow incredibly in Europe, where I live, and in the United States where I often teach. Interest in meeting and navigating inner experience more skillfully has grown hugely, popularized through secular mindfulness programs as well as Buddhist silent retreats. Encouragingly for both our personal and cultural evolution, more and more people find the need, the wish, and, crucially, the *commitment* to train their minds and free their hearts.

Meditation is an intimate engagement with our lives, not something to *do*—it is a deep familiarization with experience, irreducible to a mere technique. All the talk of *mind-training* and *mindfulness* can make meditation sound a bit, well, mind-y— which is to say, a bit mental! All the language and descriptions of "working with the mind" can exacerbate our already chronic tendency to mentalize or abstract our experience, whereas we really need to gather our attention into our immediate, visceral, *somatic* experience—into this sensory body where all experience is actually happening.

This book will lead you into the whole body of your life using embodied *presence* (the meditative quality we commonly call "mindfulness," but which we might think of here, more as "body-fulness"). However much you train your mind, meditation has to be a visceral process more than a mental exercise—if it is not grounded in the body, then there is no integration. If you are not *here*, you are lost.

Each chapter addresses some feature of this body-ful practice. Taken together, they unpack and explore Buddha's exquisite yet initially mysterious statement that *the whole universe arises and passes right here in this body*. From our sensory experience, through our instinctual drives to our mental processing, emotional reactivity, and relational patterns, we'll explore how to live more freely and love more fully—how to *inhabit* your body and your life.

This book is not another in the burgeoning collection on "how to meditate." It is a guidebook for an embodied life—an invitation to be with yourself under the microscope of meditative awareness, to meet life up close and close in—to settle into the visceral theater of *here-ness*, right where your life is playing out.

We'll also explore all the habitual obstacles to this process: the demands upon, defenses against, and distractions from our immediate, sensory life. We will examine our busyness—our screens and devices—our overly goal-oriented lives, our reliance on stimulation and entertainment, consumption and comfort—our myriad strategies of avoiding ourselves—of going *up and out* into unnecessary and unhelpful drama and disconnection.

This book will consistently invite you *in and down*—back into embodied presence. Intentionally, *attentionally* inhabiting your felt experience takes you "under your skin," beneath the descriptions, interpretations, and reactions that usually clutter the mind. Deeply embodied meditative practice is utterly transformative, beyond the prosaic vision of some mindfulness approaches—beyond stress management, beyond better sleep and being more "in the moment"—to a vision and a real possibility of a liberated life.

I've tried to write in the way I teach, in which I always have two aims. First, I want to meet you, the reader, right where you are—referencing experiences you recognize, situations you find yourself in—patterns that are all too familiarly human and ordinary, the stuff of your everyday life and mind. Second—and I know it sounds contradictory to the first point, but that is the delicate art of teaching—I want to simultaneously point you *beyond* (possibly *unimaginably beyond*) where you already are. The teachings and practices I offer, and which in turn were offered to me by my own teachers, point to a totally free human existence—free of reactivity, free of fear, free of pettiness—free to live, love, and *know* your freeness of being, unshakably. If you explore only what you already know, you end up reinforcing your own mental content. If I only point you beyond where you are, then transcendence becomes avoidance, or *spiritual bypassing*. Real transformative work happens when you do both simultaneously. You meet yourself in order to see right through *you*—and you explore your material in order to drop it.

My aim, then, is to lead you into your own life—right in, into your physical body where it all happens—into an intimacy you may have tasted occasionally or maybe have never known—into a quality of listening instead of knowing, of sensing rather than reacting—into the embrace of the whole universe, which is unfolding *here*, in this very body.

Sense yourself sitting here, just for a moment.

The feel of your feet and legs.

The gentle movement of your breathing.

Come inside, and let's explore together.

1

This Human Body

Who feels it knows it, Lord.

—BOB MARLEY

THE HUMAN CONDITION

Life is unreliable. Pain is unavoidable. All we accumulate we will lose, and all those we love will disappoint us and disappear from our lives—if we don't go first. We have a frustrating lack of control over what experience comes our way and how we react to it. It is not easy, this human life.

And yet we feel it should be easier.

We succumb to the delusion that others have it easy, imagining our friends or colleagues have somehow figured things out that we haven't. I so well remember feeling insecure or confused and that I should be different. As if my life could be perfect, if only *I* could be perfect. (No pressure!) And of course, nobody anywhere has ever managed that—and yet we keep on trying as if it were possible, exhausting ourselves in the process.

Recognizing this truth is quite relieving. All the while I imagine I should have it all figured out, that I ought to be more successful, more attractive, or more intelligent, I can't help but feel there is something wrong with me. And then of course, there must be someone to blame. Surely it is someone's fault that my life doesn't correspond to my idealized version of it. (My fault? My parents? God's? Those are, after all, the usual suspects). But human life is complex and unpredictable. When we see that life cannot possibly meet our exact wishes and preferences, we relax. We begin to forgive our human frailties and failings and to treat ourselves more gently.

We allow ourselves to be less than perfect.

In this relief, we find that imperfection is completely natural— that it is the inherent nature of having a human life. We move from reaching for perfection, to bathing in the relief at imperfection. The chef at Moulin de Chaves, the meditation retreat center where I live and teach in Southwest France, once wrote on the fridge door, quoting me from a teaching I had just given, "Freedom of being is the absence of anxiety about imperfection." She thought it was a wipeable marker, but it turned out to be indelible ink and lasted several years. Eventually however, even "permanent" ink succumbs to the infallibility of impermanence.

LOST IN THOUGHT

A journalist visiting the monastery of my early teacher Ajahn Buddhadasa asked him how he would describe the state of humanity. Ajahn's reply was, "Lost in thought."

That is the default condition for most of us, most of the time. Like James Joyce's Mr. Duffy, who "lived a short distance from his body," we are caught up in abstraction, reaction, and interpretation—lost in ideas rather than immersed in life's immediacy. We tell ourselves and each other stories about our experience (increasingly documented on Instagram or Facebook) rather than really inhabiting it. We are tense in ways we barely notice—leaving ourselves and losing ourselves until we don't know any different.

Embodied awareness is the way back home—intimacy with where and how we are right now, with what is happening and how we are meeting it. Ease and intimacy with ourselves is not only possible, it is our most natural state. Yet having spent decades developing our inner discourse, we find ourselves quite attached to it. We could blame our habitually distracted state on "modern life," and maybe particularly on the internet and the screens that increasingly fill both our work lives and leisure time. We could speculate about how disembodiment is a byproduct of increasingly urban lives and our subsequent estrangement from the natural world. But disconnection is nothing new. The habit of losing ourselves in drama and detail is as old as humanity, developing as language and culture developed, growing as the very human capacity for thought and abstraction itself grew.

We are *Homo sapiens sapiens*, beings that know that we know, that can not only experience life, but also describe our experience, refer to our experience—and abstract our experience.

So how do you come back to yourself and be at home in your experience? How do you meet the world without leaving yourself?

Relax . . . and Be Attentive

More than twenty-five centuries ago, Buddha was already pointing at how we get lost in thought and inviting us to come back. After years of ascetic practices, trying to "transcend" his body but weakening and abusing it in the process, he changed his approach after remembering resting in the shade of a tree as a teenager. He recalled both the ease and relaxation of being at home in his own skin and the alertness as he let his surroundings meet his senses. These two qualities woke him up to this essence of skillful attention: relaxing into bodily experience and being attentive to what arises.

Most of the ways we know to relax involve some way of going unconscious (having a drink, watching TV, taking a nap). And most ways we know how to focus or concentrate involve some sense of strain. We furrow our brow, screw up our face, concentrate "hard" on something we are doing. Relaxation and focus seem like opposites—if we relax, we are unfocused. If we focus, we are not relaxed.

Yet relaxation and focus can (and in meditative awareness need to) go together. In sports we call it being "in the zone." There is something deeply compelling about watching an athlete who is both totally committed and absorbed, yet also relaxed, graceful, effortless. Roger Federer is an exquisite example. Skilled musicians also show us this, focused on the melody, the rhythm, the technique, while also completely absorbed in the mood and pleasure of the music.

Sports and music show us the possibility of simultaneous relaxation and focus. Meditative awareness, though, differs in several important ways.

First, there is neither action nor goal into which these qualities are poured. In meditation we relax into and focus on simply being here—on what arises naturally rather than on what we are doing or creating. There is nothing to accomplish, nothing that should happen. We are entering into what *is* without trying to get anywhere. Hence the classic meditation adage: Nothing to do, nowhere to go, no one to be.

Second, athletes and musicians' attention is being held by strong stimuli (the running, the tennis match, the song being sung or played). Intensity attracts attention easily (people at the movies have no trouble sitting down and focusing for a couple of hours). But in meditation we are entering into the most ordinary and uncompelling elements of experience—the breathing body, sensations, and sounds. Attending to these nonstimulating elements trains the attention: it becomes steadier, subtler, more penetrating.

A third difference is that we are exploring experience for the purpose of wisdom. We meditate to be awake to the nature of experience, to see reality clearly, to understand ourselves and life in a way that is freeing. This makes meditation distinctly different from other absorbing activities. Some will say "Dance is my meditation," or "Painting is my meditation, because I get absorbed in it. I forget myself and feel one with the music, the painting, the world." That is beautiful—but it is not transformational meditation. The main feature of a transformational meditative practice is not to attain an absorption state—the main feature is wisdom. We meet experience deeply not just to feel it, but to understand our relationship to it, and in doing so to let go of the drama and tension we habitually create.

Most of us are so used to holding certain tension patterns that we don't notice them. A friend of mine was giving someone a massage, and when she lifted the person's arm, it just stayed there, stiffly. "Relax," she said. "I am relaxed," he replied (stiffly!). "What about your arm?" she asked. And then, of course, he could feel it and soften the muscles there. When attention goes somewhere, then we notice. Once we feel and understand the tension, we can soften it.

Check in right now as you are reading this.

How are the muscles in your face? Your shoulders?

If there are tensions, see if they can soften. And as you continue reading, see if you can do so while continuing to sense into bodily life.

In meditation, relaxation and focus support and enhance each other. The more we focus, the more we feel tensions and can relax them. The more we relax, the more conscious we are, and the more we notice. We become aware of subtle tensions and can let them soften, deepening the relaxation and the depth of contact with our experience, which in turn allows us to find other "nonrelaxed" zones. As well as muscular tensions we start to find energetic knots, psychological blockages, emotional holding, and more. There seems to be literally no limit to our capacity to both focus and relax. And our bodily experience is the ground for this whole exploration.

Cultivating both focus and relaxation, we meet experience more fully. We start to taste the truth of one of my favorite statements of the Buddha, one which in some ways gives us the thread and flow of this whole book:

> The entire universe
> arises and passes
> right here
> in this body.

EMBODIED ATTENTION

How important, then, that we learn to be right here, in this body! If the whole universe is showing up right here, what a tragedy if I keep missing it through the endless involvement in my own drama. Embodied awareness is the essence of meditation. Body and consciousness cannot be separated—a human body is a conscious body. Take the consciousness away and you have . . . a corpse, a lump of rotting flesh. No consciousness, no body.

If you want to be really at home in your skin, you have to embody your experience. Listening not only with your ears but with your whole being, with your cells. Listening to your sensory life closely, with care, as if to a new language—one of sensation, energy, density and space, mood and feeling, tension and relaxation.

What might that be like, right now? Reading these pages, what is it like to be sitting here? Let your attention drop for a moment into the felt sense of your experience, just as it is. Feel your lower body, and the density of sensation caused by the pressure of your buttocks and thighs on the seat, the cushion, chair, or floor.

Take your time with this. Relax into it. Feel along your arms. Feel your hands holding this book. How much tension is required to keep holding it? Obviously some, or it will drop from your grip. But are there any extra, unnecessary tensions involved? Some habitual tendency to hold yourself a little more tightly than necessary? To draw yourself into the familiar knot of self? And if so, might it soften, even a little?

Can you taste the softening? Feel the ease of letting unnecessary tension drop? Can you let focus and relaxation come together, right now? Sensing your experience, feeling what it is like—letting yourself relax.

What about your face? We often hold tension around the eyes or in the jaw. As you explore, feel from the inside. Invite everything to relax, but without demanding, without expecting any particular result.

See if you can settle a little more fully into the felt experience of sitting here, reading these words, meeting life from inside experience.

INSIDE EXPERIENCE

In the old Buddhist texts, evocative language points us clearly into the intimacy of meditative awareness. The texts distinguish clearly between embodied (*yoniso*) and disembodied (*ayoniso*) attention (*manisikara*).

If you are familiar with yogic tradition and language, you may recognize *yoni** as meaning "vagina," though here it more precisely means "womb." Embodied attention, then, is literally "from the womb"—that is, grounded down in the lower belly. While mostly our attention is disembodied, disconnected, cut off from the visceral immediacy of our lives, here we are asked to inhabit our center of gravity, to be awake in our womb. Those without the certain female organs may be feeling left out here, but we are talking about an energetic womb, not a biological one—felt as the deepest place in us. The womb is the source of life both literally (we all come directly from the womb)and energetically; this is the center of embodied, or we might say *em-bellied*, attention.

A woman of about thirty-five, a successful academic with a busy mind, was on retreat with me recently. We explored together how she could drop her attention down into her lower body, using her breathing to settle her attention in her abdomen. Initially she felt nothing, and so I encouraged her to rest her hands gently over her belly as she sat, the touch provoking some warm sensation there. As the retreat progressed, she began to feel a deep presence in her womb. Unfamiliar with what she called "my womb speaking to me," she thought this must be a hitherto repressed longing for children welling up in her, but as she stayed with it, she realized her belly was energetically "coming to life." For the first time, she was able to be present right inside her physical experience. She began to feel

* In Sanskrit, *yoni* can be used in reference to any part of the female reproductive system.

a powerful sense of confidence, which could be seen in how she stood taller and walked more gracefully. She was starting to inhabit her body, to lead with her belly, to experience life without leaving herself.

DON'T "BE MINDFUL OF . . ."

Meditation is pretty mainstream these days. Mindfulness in particular has made various practices and teachings widely accessible, and many people have become familiar with "watching the breath," "observing sensation," and "being mindful of" moment-by-moment experience. Words like *mind, attention, consciousness, mindfulness* even, have disembodied connotations and can reinforce an overly mentalized way of practicing: I "observe" my experience as if from a distance. If I am "watching" my breath, then I am outside of it. If I am "mindful of" experience, then who or what is standing outside the experience to be mindful? The language reinforces the sense of a predominantly mental discipline. Maybe this is inevitable. We are indeed training our minds through directing our attention and exploring our consciousness, but we need to dissolve that gap between observer and observed, seer and seen. We need to bring our attention in and down, countering our usual habit of going up and out.

The old texts reveal how crucial is this embodied approach to a successful meditation practice. The more-or-less standard translation for the Pali *sati* is "mindfulness." It is way too late now to try and change that, but personally I find that translation a little clumsy. Only slightly tongue-in-cheek, I might propose for this book that we think of it more as "body-fullness"! I personally prefer the term "presence," which is both etymologically closer (*sati* literally means to recall or gather one's attention, to remember where one is, to be present in the midst of one's experience). Importantly, there is no equivalent in the texts to "being mindful of" what is happening. The grammar is such that one either "enters into" or "establishes oneself in" *sati* (presence, mindfulness).

How might that affect the way you practice? Trying to be "mindful of" my experience, I remain "the watcher," the one being mindful. I abstract myself from the experience. What if we abandoned this tiresome watcher, controller, and commentator? What if, right now, you don't try to *be mindful of* what is happening? Instead, enter into experience. Feel your way into what is happening rather than trying to observe it from the position of a watcher. When I give meditation instructions, I use language that encourages people to be intimate with, to sense into, to inhabit experience—all ways of expressing a "knowing from the inside," another important phrase from the traditional texts.

The fundamentals of Buddhist meditation come from the Mahasatipatthana Sutta (The Greater Discourse on Establishing Presence). In it, Buddha outlines in great depth and detail the four specific areas of experience to contemplate:

- *Kayanupassana*—bodily experience
- *Vedananupassana*—the feel or tone of experience (pleasant, unpleasant, or neutral)
- *Cittanupassana*—the momentary coloring of mental/emotional experience
- *Dhammanupassana*—the nature of experience

The four areas build on each other. We don't move from bodily experience to some other aspect. We establish presence in bodily experience, as the foundation for meeting all experience. Or said another way, all experience is embodied experience. This is underlined by the recurring encouragement through all four aspects, repeated at the end of every section, to know experience from the inside. Knowing bodily experience *not* through an idea or image of "my body, this body"—but knowing the body in the body, knowing the breathing in the breathing, the feel of the experience inside the experience. This clear emphasis is the ground of embodied practice—as such I'll encourage you again and again to feel into where you are, to sense into your experience as it is. Because this is how a genuinely alive, embodied practice will develop.

This is how embodied wisdom will grow and flourish.

This is how you'll find ease and spaciousness in being right where you are.

Embodied Presence

Fully inhabiting experience, you notice when tensions or reactivity arise and can meet them without overreaching into unnecessary drama. Embodied presence feels relaxed and open, easily contented. I learned this by example from my teachers.

In 1990, shortly after discovering and engaging with Buddhist practices, I met a Himalayan hermit called Sukhanta Giri, whom most people called simply Babaji. I was nineteen years old. I had come to India with a one-way ticket and no luggage, searching for depth and meaning, inspired by images and fantasies of mystical India, driven by adolescent wanderlust and existential angst.

I had just completed a ten-day meditation course in Dharamsala, the Himalayan hill town in Northern India that is home to the His Holiness the Dalai Lama and the Tibetan Government-in-Exile. The teachings and practices during the course affected me profoundly, and about twenty minutes into the first teachings on the first evening, in a moment of great exhilaration, I felt clearly that I had spent my whole life looking for these teachings. Here was a way to explore consciousness—a way to wake up to my habits and beliefs, to get out of my own way and let life in! Here was a way to align with generations of other people who had also felt restless and dissatisfied with the usual conventions of education-career-marriage-retirement-death, a way to train my mind and free my heart, to wake up and live more fully, more fluidly, more freely.

It was like finding water in the desert, and at the end of the course, I resolved to make like a yogi and find a cave. That was the real way to meditate, right? I had no blanket, and I had no cookstove or pot. I didn't know how I was going to eat or keep warm. But I did know that serious yogis went into the mountains, so while terrified at the thought, I set off the day after the retreat in search of my "cave in the snow," or at least in the forest beneath the snow line.

To simplify a somewhat melodramatic story, I never made it to the cave. I bumped into an old sadhu (Hindu renunciate) on the road out of town, a man whom I had met and spent time with some months previously in the Rajasthani desert a thousand kilometers away. We greeted each other and he asked me where I was headed.

"To a cave, to meditate," I replied, grandiosely. In testament to his great compassion, I don't think he actually rolled his eyes. I like to think he appreciated my youthful enthusiasm, though also no doubt saw its folly. He himself had come to India from Fiji at nineteen and had never gone back again. He carried a long white stick with many pieces of cloth tied to it, and when I had once asked him what they were for, he replied, "Each one is a telephone number for God. I keep on dialing, dialing. Any moment—God answer!"

Shaking his head paternally, Fiji Baba told me not to go in search of a cave. He instead pointed me up the hill and across the river, into a small valley where he said one "Bengali Baba" was living, who had a hut and kept a *dhuni*, the fireplace that sadhus keep as part of their practice, and would probably let me stay. He wrote me a note of introduction in Hindi, probably "Please look after this poor deluded boy"—and I followed his directions through a beautiful cedar-scented forest valley to a small orange gate with the *AUM* sign written above. I found Babaji sitting at his fireplace, greeted him with palms together, and handed him the note. He nodded, pointed to a bare room, and said I could stay three days. I put down my small bag—and spent most of the next three years there with him.

Babaji and I didn't converse so much. His English was limited and my Hindi was still poor at the time. He encouraged me to develop and deepen the meditation practice I had already started. We sat by the fire together, worked in the garden, fetched firewood. He cooked and I washed the dishes. Others came and went, staying shorter or longer times. People often ask what he taught me. I reply that he didn't teach anything, but that I learned much.

Truly, Babaji didn't teach anything—but he gave a gentle, gracious, and generous attention to each gesture he made, every task he undertook, everyone he received at the ashram. The way he unscrewed the tea jar was a teaching. How he kneaded chapati dough and turned the wood in the fire—the way he washed the spinach, checked the rice for stones, fed leftovers to the local dogs—all these things communicated a quality of presence, of care, of intimacy with life. The way he listened, the way he laughed, the way he scolded villagers who came to settle disputes—correcting, advising and admonishing them without ever belittling or shaming them.

Babaji didn't teach me anything, but he showed me how to attend to experience. My Buddhist teachers told me how to meditate, but Babaji showed me how to live. My Buddhist teachers taught me about mindfulness; Babaji showed me what presence was. And what he showed me, most of all, was that it was possible. That presence wasn't something to "attain"—some exalted plateau to reach. That it didn't depend on some particular depth of meditation or some special experience, but simply on the quality of attention, moment by moment. An attention that is intimate, generous, relaxed—in short: embodied.

Windows Can Paint Themselves

One time I decided to repaint the ashram windows. I took a bus to town and bought paint, brushes, sandpaper. The old red paint was sun-bleached, dull, and peeling, and I worked eagerly, excited by the twin expectations of shining new windows and my teacher's approval.

Babaji shook his head. "Your problem" he said, "is that you're busy painting the windows." Er, yes. That's the idea. But what he was inviting me to do was to come back to myself. To return to the immediacy of the painting itself and to give up straining for the result. My task, I found, was not to paint the windows, but rather to see the wood. To feel the brush in my hand. To notice when I started to get ahead of myself and to come back. To simply take care of each brushstroke. And in that way, as Babaji said, "the windows can paint themselves."

It's a bit like that, writing this book. My very kind and extremely patient publishers have been encouraging me for a few years, but I could neither find the time nor the real motivation for a while. Now that I have finally signed a contract and committed to it, writing a whole book seems way too daunting. But of course, that is not my task. I just need to take care of this section, find a way to express what I want to right here. And sure enough (at least this is what I'm counting on with about 20 percent written so far), eventually, the book will have written itself.

Don't Leave Yourself

Ajahn Mun, another famous Thai meditation master, used to give the instruction, "Never let your mind leave your body." If that seems too much to ask, then how about this: every time you notice that your mind has left your body really notice that. Notice that feeling of being "up and out" of yourself, of being caught in some abstraction. Sense into the inevitable tensions that have arisen through your attention having been hijacked . . . and let it all go. You return by coming "in and down," by re-embodying your experience.

Where is your attention now? It might well be "up and out" on the page you are reading. That's what we do. We feel that to connect to something, we need to go "out there" to it. But fundamentally, there is no "out there." The book, the page, the reading, the understanding (hopefully)—it's all here. Here in awareness. Here in experience. So again (and don't worry about the repetition, you'll need to do this several billion times), how about coming in and down? It is counterintuitive to a mind (your mind, my mind, everyone's mind) that has been conditioned to go out to meet experience, but actually, you don't need to go anywhere. Ever.

Come in and down. Feel your arms and legs. The weight of your legs on your seat. Stay where you are. Settle into your direct, visceral experience. And notice that you can still see "the world around you." That you can still read these words. You can let the world come to you instead of going after it. You can let experience rise up to meet you where you are, instead of losing yourself in its pursuit.

YOU ARE ALREADY HERE

When we first start really noticing, it's astonishing to see where the mind goes—how often and how compellingly we're caught up in all kinds of stuff and how so much of it is basically just rubbish. Like an automatic content-generator, we spew forth an endless stream of habit-formed thinking: partial recollections of what has happened previously, vague anticipations of what we hope or fear will happen next, habitual commentary on what is happening now. It can seem impossibly difficult, like it would take an unimaginable amount of mindfulness, to be constantly present in the face of all those pulls on our attention.

But practice nevertheless, and you'll notice something crucially important: It is *not* being present that is such hard work, it is all the departures—the endless demands, defenses, and distractions—that take so much energy. We are so habituated to all this mental activity, that it feels normal. But if every time you notice that your attention has gone off somewhere, you sense what is happening in your body, you'll start to notice the subtle tensions of leaning out of yourself. You'll feel how being lost in thought is inherently stressful as you recognize the inevitable physical tension of fabricating, feeding, and then reacting to whatever stimuli you've gotten involved with. And then you'll see that you return to presence not by an act of will, not by forcing your attention back to some elusive "present moment," but by recognizing and releasing these tensions. Returning to presence, in other words, is mostly and most simply about relaxing.

Life's immediacy is way more powerful than all your little fixations. However deep you go down the rabbit hole of your own thinking, sooner or later life wakes you up to the fact that you are *here*. One student memorably noticed this when he was trying so hard to be present, trying to let go of all his thoughts and come back to his breath, and feeling increasingly tired and frustrated. Eventually, it was all too much and he just gave up. He opened his eyes, watching the raindrops run down the nearby window. And like the Buddha's recollection of lying under the tree, he realized that he was here. Aware. Watching raindrops instead of breaths, but at the same time present in his body. It was suddenly obvious that he didn't need to *do anything* to be here.

Do you need to do anything right now, to be here? Wherever you direct your attention, here is your experience. You can see, and know you are seeing. Breathe, and feel you are breathing. Read and understand these words, and be inside the experience as it is happening.

You don't *do* awareness. Instead of the effort to be present, there is effortless presence every time you relax your contracted, fixated attention.

With some sincerity and commitment (called practice), this can become your consistent, near constant home.

2

The Uncomfortable Body

---◆---

SUFFERING IN SILENCE

Sitting quietly (often called meditation) can be the most sublimely peaceful experience. It offers the most refined way to really rest into nondoing—an opportunity to truly relax not only your muscles, but also your nervous system, your breathing, your thought world. Meditation can be a moment of bathing deeply in true silence, stillness, and peace.

And . . . (more commonly) meditation can be filled with restlessness and agitation, boredom and dullness—endless, fruitless wandering thoughts—and after a while, increasing physical discomfort.

I suffered a lot when I began to meditate.

I was very idealistic. I felt that as I was young—still a teenager—I ought to be supple and able to sit easily, my legs folded Buddha-like one on top of the other for long periods of time. I couldn't. It hurt like hell, but I felt I *should be able to*, and so as I say, I suffered a lot. I suffered from the pain in my poor crunched-up legs. I suffered from trying to look like Buddha instead of just following his instructions. I suffered from the idea that I shouldn't be suffering, and I suffered from judging myself for giving myself a hard time about not being able to sit still. Poor me!

Someone once went to see the teacher at the end of a retreat, both to thank her and to ask a question: "I have really appreciated the retreat, but my legs hurt so much, sitting so long in meditation. If I continue to practice, will it hurt less?" The teacher smiled, brightly. "Probably not," she replied, "But after a while, you won't mind so much."

Actually, she was exaggerating a little. As we get used to sitting in meditation, whether on the floor or a chair, things do start to ease, open, and soften. But the far more significant shift is that of our relationship with the discomfort. We learn to relax into it—to stop fussing, fighting, and freaking out about it. And that is where the real ease comes from. When we sense into physical discomfort (*pain!*), we find it usually consists mostly of heat and density. Sensations that are prickly, warm, pressurized, intense, tight. Much of our discomfort is quite bearable when we attend to the sensations themselves, but becomes too much for us when we get carried away by our reactivity to it.

Sitting in the Fire

When I was at Wat Suan Mokh, Ajahn Buddhadasa's monastery in Thailand, there was a huge wall mural of a great fire, painted by one of the monks. In it, a wild, green, coiled serpent stared out with yellow eyes blazing, fangs bared, and forked tongue spitting aggressively forward. Painted on the tip of its tongue, right in the midst of all the heat and danger and intensity . . . was a monk, seated in meditation—eyes gently closed, a half smile on his face.

This image was a great support and reminder to me. I sure felt the fire in my legs, and my own mind often felt like that snake. I started to learn how to lean in to my experience, to listen to the discomfort without adding to it, to sit in the fire and be gentle in the face of intensity.

As I settled into meditation practice, I learned how to care for my experience without making a drama out of it. What we call awareness is more than just attention. It is an attitude that is generous and gentle, that allows what arises to actually be felt. The sense is this: If this is what life is presenting right now, let me be respectful enough to really attend to it, to care enough that I can find out what is needed and how to respond.

Attend in this way, and you'll find to your surprise that the discomfort that you have so disliked and pushed against might actually be your friend—and your teacher.

No Pain, No Gain

I think I first heard "No pain, no gain" in *Fame*, the 1980s TV show. The phrase can be used to justify all kinds of unhelpful masochism, but there is a grain of truth to it. No authentic transformative practice can avoid confronting pain. I know that doesn't sound very glamorous. It's not what we put on the posters when we are advertising a weeklong meditation retreat:

> **A Week of Pain**
> *7 tortuous days of sitting*
> with your uncomfortable body
> and uncooperative mind.
> Sign up here.

And of course, that's not the whole story. There is joy and love, expansion and peace, depths of relaxation and insight. But nevertheless, to a significant extent, for most of us it is in the crucible of working with our difficulties that our practice takes root and begins to blossom. Nobody ever undertook a transformative journey because everything was perfectly wonderful in their lives. No, we come *because of* the difficulties we experience and because we intuit that it doesn't have to be like this. Something in us recognizes the possibility for a more fluid existence and knows we need to get close to ourselves and really listen.

One Thing Only?

There is a key statement by the Buddha that reads curiously at first glance: "I teach one thing and one thing only: Suffering and the resolution of suffering."

We might legitimately ask (especially as he has made a point of emphasizing it as one thing and one thing only), why he then goes on to mention two things—suffering and its resolution?

It is because they are found *in the same place*. We don't escape from pain. We don't lift out of it and float off into the Pure Land, any more than we are likely to levitate off our meditation cushion.

We meet it. We turn toward it. That is where the proverbial rubber meets the road—where your awareness meets your life. We all spend time, some decades at least, trying to outrun our discomforts and defenses, but at some point, we realize that we've "been down that road before." And it's a dead end. That's when we turn toward presence and encounter ourselves—our habits, our fears, our resistance.

Two Kinds of Pain

There are two kinds of pain, and the first you can't do much about.

The body ages. We get sick, feel uncomfortable, and wear out in various unpleasant and unglamorous ways, considerably faster than we would like. Moisturize as much as you like, but gravity is going to win. The upside is that today, right now, is as good as it gets. It's an irrevocable decline from here, so make the most of today—you will never be this young again.

The second kind of pain is in the extra layers that apparently we just love to add on. The complaints, the self-pity, the blame. *Poor me, why me, why now, why this?* The struggle and resistance, the fight and the flight, the myriad ways we squirm and struggle against reality. And this is what is *really hard* to be with. This is where we get busy creating the friction.

"Pain is inevitable," says the classic Buddhist aphorism, "suffering is optional." This second kind of pain then, we can do a *lot* about, but we have to do it by hanging out at the site of our discomfort—by *inhabiting* it. In a story about the "wise fool" Mullah Nasruddin, he is found one night by his friend searching under the streetlight outside his house. He explains he has lost his keys, but after some time looking, there is no sign of them. "Mullah, are you sure you lost them here?" asks his friend. "No, I lost them in the garden," says Nas-ruddin. "But it is much easier to search here in the light."

That's how it is with uncomfortable experience, whether physi-cal, emotional, or situational. We just want it to be different. I want to be with my experience—but not *this* experience! We would rather look where it is more comfortable, but that's why we're reminded: *Suffering and its resolution: one thing and one thing only.*

You have to meet the one to know the other.

Let the Bell Ring

In Buddhist monasteries, there is plenty of encouragement to turn toward pain. Ajahn Chah apparently used to ask people with a big smile, "So, how are you suffering today?" My teacher Ajahn Poh used to sit unmoving for hours on end. While I shuffled and wriggled, went outside to do walking meditation, came back in to sit again, he would just be there—steady, even, peaceful. Watching him sit like a mountain gave me great encouragement. His example showed me it was possible to actually turn to my own discomfort—not only my knee pain, back pain, shoulder pain, but all the extra layers I was adding on top—the drama and denial, the fussing and fighting.

I started to feel just how hard I was resisting my experience. I would be waiting, praying for the bell to end the sitting. But in imag-ining the bell as the bringer of peace, I made my current experience unbearable. And curiously, when it finally rang, I often felt great relief *even before I changed my posture.* Did the bell possess some magical power to ease all suffering? No, but as soon as I heard it ring, I let go. I gave up resisting. When I stopped pushing back at my dis-comfort, suddenly it was OK to be there.

So I started giving myself permission to "let the bell ring" inter-nally, at any moment. Again and again and again. OK, it's over. You can stop. Stop resisting. Stop meditating. Stop pulling and pushing. Stop trying to manage experience and just feel it as it is. Feel, and soften. Feel, and allow. Feel, and stay there. And my relationship to that discomfort started to change.

Meditation teaches us that it's OK to feel what's here—and not just OK, but profoundly relieving. Otherwise, it's like we're pushing against a coiled spring. And the harder you push, the more it seems like the spring is pushing back. And we've been pushing for so long, we barely even notice we're doing it or how much energy it is consuming. And so you'd better keep pushing, because you can feel how much tension is there, and you wouldn't want that to release, because . . .

Because what? What would happen if you stopped resisting the spring? *Boing!* It would release all its energy . . . and be done. All the while we're pushing, we remain convinced we need to keep pushing. Yet as soon as we stop, *relief.*

Life gives us many, many opportunities to stop pushing. And each time we do, we have the opportunity to *taste* the relief. To let it in, so that our cells get familiar with the ease of letting go. To be as clear as possible that it is not worth pushing against the spring. It will only keep pushing back.

When you notice you are tense around your eyes, let them soften. When you realize you are moving a little more quickly than you need to, slow down. When you are impatient to speak, train yourself to feel the impatience, and then drop it. When you are fighting with reality, pushing against the spring . . . Stop.

And repeat as above, several million times or so.

Presence Is Pleasant

Softening, slowing, somatizing. Reconnecting in this way is a direct path not only to cultivating embodied presence, but also to *enjoying* it. The body doesn't need to be a source of discomfort, impatience, jitteriness, or numbness. Most essentially, presence is pleasant. For a tangible example of what I mean, tense your muscles for a moment. Tense along your arms and legs, lift your perineum, and scrunch up your face a little.

I won't leave you there for too long, but feel what it is like.

Notice not only how uncomfortable it is, but also how much work it takes and how dense you feel—how solid and separate from the world around you.

And now . . . relax. Let your muscles soften, and feel *that*. Notice the quality of the relaxation. The *relief*—how suddenly easeful and effortless it is to be here, pleasant to be in your skin.

And that is just the gross, muscular form of relaxation. As we enter into the body more fully, we will also find levels of subtler relaxation—energetic, emotional, psychological, and existential.

For myself, I was so surprised when I started to taste this freeness of the body that I didn't quite trust it. I liked it, I enjoyed it, I loved it. But I was also quite full of Buddhist ideas about suffering, and I felt somehow that all this pleasantness was cheating! Then I came across a textual passage where Buddha speaks about a skilled contemplative being one who (as the Suttas say) "makes their own pleasure," through "the rapture and pleasure" of embodied awareness "drenching, steeping, filling, and pervading this body."

You can be genuinely at ease in your skin—at rest in your experience, your nervous system pervaded by pleasure.

This is the promise of embodied awareness, and the very real possibility for all of us.

3

The Instinctual Body

Whose Life Is It Anyway?

We didn't decide on this life for ourselves. We didn't choose our gender, nationality, or family. We don't recall our beginning or know anything about how or when our life will end—yet we call it "my life," implying an ownership and control we just don't have. Like images on a movie screen, a flow of impressions passes through consciousness out of which we construct memories, plans, and a narrative to fit. And just as we get caught up in the onscreen action in the cinema, the drama seems very real and personal until we turn our attention around and look at where the projections are coming from.

We have a *lot* of material out of which to generate projected content. Our very human conditioning is layered on top of a mammalian brain and biology, which in turn has developed from a more basic reptilian form. And finally, here we are. Millions upon millions of years of evolution to produce *you*!

With our humanity incorporating our evolutionary past, we experience the same instincts as all of life: to survive, to reproduce, and to bond with others. The survival drive, the sex drive, and the social drive are biologically programmed through all our evolutionary layers. We seek, often unconsciously, to act them out and gratify them, but it's never enough. Like a hamster on its wheel, earnestly convinced it is getting somewhere, the endless, cyclic pursuit of desire-gratification is spurred by the idea that we are moving toward some kind of contentment. But where is it? Nobody ever just got so well gratified that they retired into permanent satisfaction. We are invited to explore and understand the drive for satisfaction, rather then just endlessly pursuing it.

The religious traditions have traditionally attempted the opposite approach, variously endeavoring to escape, suppress, deny, hide, and transcend our instinctual desires. But you cannot transcend your biology, and we see the fallout from trying to in the pedophilia of Catholic priests and the abuse of money, sex, and power by a depressingly long list of gurus.

If we are not awake to these primitive and powerful drives, then they pull at our attention, stimulate our physiology, quite literally *driving* us around. So what do we find when we enter into and explore our instinctual lives?

THE INSTINCTUAL DRIVES

The table below shows different features of the instincts. They are all familiar to us, yet we may recognize a dominant orientation. Each has a very specific preoccupying loop, reinforcing its sense of importance like a vortex. The more we go around in our particular version of the loop, the stronger the pattern becomes.

The survival drive shows up most often as basic anxiety about getting one's needs met. A "survival type" likes to have the cupboards well stocked, wants to feel prepared for any eventuality. The main fixation is on oneself. What do I need to do to feel OK? To be safe, secure, and comfortable? The preoccupying loop is one of self-concern and self-protection. The hoped-for destination is one of self-sufficiency: "If I can get things arranged safely and comfortably for myself, *then I'll feel OK.*"

Overview of the Instinctual Drives: I will survive, I want you, and I need to be successful

Instinct	Survival	Sex	Social
Preoccupying loop / Inner relationship	Self to self	Self to other	Self to world
Neurotic version (ego-deficient)	Is there enough for me?	Am I enough for you?	Am I doing enough in the world?
Narcissistic version (ego-inflated)	I deserve more than enough. There should be enough for me.	Are you enough for me?	Does the world appreciate me enough?
Fixation	Security, comfort	Intimacy, romance	Success, approval
Common areas of fixation	Money Food Doing things my way "Having my space" Safety, protection Possessiveness	Emotional drama Intense relationships Blame Idealization / demonization Complex relationship with authority figures	Ambition Concern for self-image Need to impress Concern about being center of attention, either shying from (neurotic) or seeking out (narcissistic)
Persistent doubt	Am I OK?	Will you make me feel OK?	Do they think I'm OK?
Pathological fixation (area of abuse / attempt to control)	Money: control over conditions	Sex: control over another	Power: control over a group

For a "sexual type," the preoccupation is with relationship. Focused on the *special one*, when the sex drive dominates, relationships are intense, the biggest thing in life. The anxiety is all about you and me: Will you keep me safe? Will you always love me? Will you give me what I want? Hey, why aren't you listening to me? The loop is between self and significant other. The hope/delusion is, "If I can love you well and get you to love me perfectly, *then I'll feel OK*."

The "social type" casts their net a little wider. Networkers, social-ites, and raconteurs—the preoccupation when the social drive domi-nates is with the world in general. *How do I appear to them? Can they see me? Are they impressed by me? What do I need to do to get their attention?* The (futile) hope here is, "If I can somehow get enough approval and admiration of others, *then I'll feel OK.*"

We are powerfully conditioned to play out these different drives, personally and culturally. Advertising is constantly waving at them, activating their primitive pull by promising visions of how to be more comfortable (survival), more attractive (sexual), and more successful (social).

The instincts drive many cultural forces. The survival drive, attuned to threat and afraid of change, is behind the reactionary fear of the "dangerous other," which is why homophobia, xenophobia, racism, and so on, as well as being aggressive (and regressive), always have something pathetic and insecure behind them. Cultural expressions of the sex drive give us everything from robot sex dolls to the happily-ever-after romantic fulfillment motif expressed in so many movies and songs. And the social drive plays out very clearly now in social media, with the need to be seen and approved of, increasingly measured in click-likes, shares, and numbers of followers. (I'm @martinaylward on Instagram, by the way!)

WHO'S DRIVING?

If you slow down and refrain for a moment from acting on your instincts, two things become possible. First, you can start to actually feel your habitual response mechanism. You can recognize the sense of lack or need that arises through feeling hungry (survival), or horny (sexual), or lonely (social). You can feel the pull at your attention, the attempt to go somewhere, get something (or someone) to try to briefly satisfy the drive. Second, the slowing allows you to find a space between the arising of the desire and your usual reaction. Here in this gap, wisdom and awareness can intervene.

In a meditation retreat, this gap is created by the environment. With little opportunity to gratify our drives, the situation invites us instead to explore them. Our basic survival needs are well cared for, though we might still find ourselves hoping to get comfortable or worrying about our sleep or whether there will be enough lunch. Retreat also manages the sex drive through the agreement to leave everyone their own space and solitude, and this becomes a mirror for any fantasy and sexual energy that arises. The social drive is also checked by being in silence. This can feel quite challenging and isolating for some, showing us how we often use social contact to reach out for approval or reassurance.

THE SURVIVAL DRIVE

For many people around the world, there is a daily question of actual survival—of having enough to eat today, of having shelter and being safe from attack. But even if we have fortunate material circumstances, the drive will still show up—obsessing about comfort or safety for instance. In fact, the further removed we are from genuine survival needs, the more neurotic and petty we can get around the drive. You can see this clearly with food—the wealthier the neighborhood, the more obsessive the dietary fads and fixations.

It also plays out in meditation centers. The more "perfect" the place is, and the more helpful and lovely the staff are in responding to people's requests . . . the more requests keep coming. You can measure them in the number of notes on the pinboard.

Very basic circumstances sometimes show us the wisdom of letting go. For eighteen years, 1991–2009, I spent every January on retreat in the Thai Monastery in Bodh Gaya, India. The first nine were as a student on the retreat, and the next nine years were teaching it. These retreats were the highlight of my year, meditating right in the place where Buddha sat under the Bodhi Tree, but nothing about the monastery could be described as comfortable. Sixty men slept and snored and farted together on straw mats in the temple basement, occasionally waking to find rats eating our soap or pulling straw out of our mats, or, in one case, gnawing the dead skin off of a guy's toes. The women had it no better—eight of them in each small room and another twenty on the floor of a long veranda. The meditation hall was cramped, the cushions were few, old, and lumpy, and the whole place was damp and infested with mosquitoes. Once a week, Anil the "latrine-*wallah*" would empty the septic tank, which was outside the door to the meditation hall, and we would meditate to the sound and the stench of the bucket splashing down into the pit, being hauled up full of our excrement, and poured into the open gutter to run off to . . . who knows where.

Some came to the retreat straight from the United States or Europe, having been encouraged by Christopher Titmuss who was leading the retreats, to come to the source of Buddha's teaching and to marinate awhile in Mother India's unique atmosphere. Faced with such simple conditions, something interesting would happen to the usual concerns about discomfort or inconvenience: After the initial shock, there were very few notes or requests. When it is very clear to us that there is just no chance to make the conditions comfortable, something can free up. We might find our capacity to surrender is greater than we knew: to let go of our control is to enlarge our comfort zone, to find out that one can abide freely, whether comfortable or not. When the option is there, we'll fuss and choose. When it is not, we accept what is offered. Monasteries use the devices of simplicity and austerity to strip away our endless preferencing.

There is a beautiful line in Hermann Hesse's *Siddhartha*, when the eponymous hero leaves his ascetic yogic practices and comes to town to look for a job. Asked about his "workplace skills," he says, "I can sit, I can fast, and I can wait." That describes a free relationship to the survival drive. You would like to be comfortable, and you can feel hunger arising, but you can sit, you can fast, and you can wait. You can attune to conditions as they are and not fuss and freak out about them. Neither a prisoner to your instincts nor trying to "transcend" them (after all, you never transcend biology!), you can simply know them arising and passing.

THE SEX DRIVE

Obviously, a lot of energy goes into sex. I don't mean only the act, (which also takes energy!) but the whole complex of attraction, merging, fantasizing, flirting, seduction, and intimacy. It is a powerful practice even for one day to note how often your thought, speech, or action is dictated by some attempt to attract or seduce or merge with another—to be loved, accepted, praised, or comforted as if your life, or at least your well-being in that moment, depended on it.

Of the three instincts, the sex drive is the easiest to notice, partly because of the strong physical sensations that draw our attention, but also because there is such a clear focus. It is like a kind of tunnel vision where everything else in the universe vanishes and the love-object pulls our attention into a vortex of obsession and need.

Poetry and art, lust and longing are all born out of the sex drive. Betrayal, heartbreak, blame, and abuse, too—as well as great intimacy, love, and healing. There is a huge chunk of human experience in there, which is why the romantic ideal is the leitmotif of popular culture. And mostly, this powerful, primitive urge is operating in us more or less blindly. No wonder it can get messy.

In spiritual teachings, sex is often frustratingly and unhelpfully left out. The message in Buddhism, as in most other religious traditions, tends to be, "Er, celibacy is the ideal. Failing that, lifelong monogamy. Now let's not talk about it any more." Some of us grow up with strong messages that sex is shameful and bad. Butch Hancock wryly describes learning from his Texas Christian upbringing that, "sex is the most awful, filthy thing on earth, and you should save it for someone you love."

Meditative investigation opens up the space where we neither need to act out a sexual urge nor suppress it. We welcome it. We allow the heat and the longing, the vivid imagery that might play out, and we stay curious so we can feel the drive and where it is pointing us.

I remember a meditation retreat where I was really burning up with sexual desire. On one hand was the frustration of having no way to actualize all my lurid fantasies, and on the other, the unsuccessful attempt to turn away from the lust and quiet my mind. I had broken my leg a month earlier, and my teacher suggested a link between the

lust and the injury. As I let myself feel the energy behind the fantasies, I saw the attempt to compensate for my situation. The fantasy
was an attempt to feel powerful, virile, and in control when my circumstances were actually the opposite, as I was physically weakened,
using crutches and dependent on the assistance of others.

I learned an important lesson—where there is obsessiveness in
how we reach out for another, it is a sure sign we are trying to compensate for some insecurity. The reaching might be for sex, or reassurance, or validation, but when I say, "I need you to make me feel OK,"
it is because I don't trust that I have that quality myself. This becomes
a self-fulfilling projection, because the more I'm hoping you will save
me, the more I'm looking at your qualities instead of my own. When
we explore instead of act out, we let go of the object of our longing
and turn toward the longing itself. The ideas and imagery are all outward focused, but the desire itself is happening *here*, in awareness.

Indulging the fantasy, compelling though it is, quickly becomes
frustrating and exhausting, with so much energy going into something fundamentally unreal. Turn instead to the embodied experience, and you suddenly feel the huge amount of *energy* in the sex
drive. The energy itself is totally meet-able, feel-able—it is enlivening, delicious, erotic.

The "erotic" is important if we are to live freely. Everything that is
felt, tasted, and touched has a sense of intimacy and delicacy. We are
constantly being kissed by experience, in erotic relationship with all of
sensory life: birdsong, the dew on the grass, the gentle movement of
breathing. At the heart of the sex drive is the longing for intimacy—
uniting with and dissolving into something outside of ourselves. And
that is the essence of meditative practice, to pour ourselves into life
and let life pour into us. In this dimension all of life is sex. All of life
interpenetrates. Everything—using Thich Nhat Hanh's phrase—
inter-is; our intimacy is with sky and earth and all of existence.

To realize and take that in is to "enlighten" the sex drive. Intimacy becomes increasingly available, and refined, as we open up this
portal within the instinct.

When you get horny, let yourself feel the heat and vitality of the sexual charge, the beauty of the depth of longing that is there. It may arise as sexual fantasy—a desire for somebody real or imagined—or equally as some other form of longing—for listening, holding, care. It may be behind your love of chocolate or music or anything else in which you seek to absorb yourself. Letting the longing be felt is the way in, to your own experience and to *inter-being* with all things.

THE SOCIAL DRIVE

We all want to be appreciated. It's natural. We want the world to reflect us back to ourselves and feel validated. When we look carefully, we see that most essentially, we want to belong fully enough to relax—to let down our defenses in knowing ourselves as part of the fabric of life. This *is* our true nature—we *inter-are* with all things, but when we don't really know this, we inevitably expend much anxious effort negotiating our relationship with the world—trying to dissolve the gap between *life*, which seems to be out there, and little ol' me in here.

So we posture and present, evaluate our performance, measure ourselves against colleagues or family or anyone or anything who will keep the familiar relationship going.

As I recounted previously, I first started exploring the instincts in monasteries and meditation retreats, which might seem remote from contemporary life. But despite the silence and "spiritual atmosphere," it is the same stuff playing out, because "wherever you go . . . there you are." Whatever the environment, we are still confronted by our own mind and its tendencies.

We can recognize our concern with social approval in moments of self-consciousness and embarrassment or equally in moments where we actively want people's attention. Children express these two movements transparently. They will cover their eyes as if it blocks out the scrutiny of the world: "I don't want to be seen." Equally, they seek attention when they want approval, "Mommy, Daddy, look at me!" We all want to be loved and cherished—by our family, our community, by the whole world, ideally. That is hard work, trying to arrive at some place in life where everybody just loves me and thinks I'm great and then I will *really* be OK.

Again, the invitation is to watch it play out and to feel the need, the drive, the anxiety as it shows up in your body. We might recognize the judge and jury we've created in the disguise of our family, or colleagues, or whoever is in our social setting, imagining what they think of us, then trying to live up to our own projections. That is one uncomfortable and strained way to live—and yet it is a primary orientation, driving us around.

Feeling into the anxiety, we recognize it as a projection and feel the stress involved in it, learning to leave it alone and let it pass by. We step outside the projection into the ease and dignity of our lived experience right now—nothing to get or get rid of. Present, embodied, intimate with, yet not embroiled in experience. An old Zen master once pointed to living freely with the social drive: "When in company, act as if you are alone. When alone, behave as if in the presence of an honored guest."

When we look into the drives, we find them activated by insecurity—seeking outside ourselves for validation of our OK-ness as if we could capture it and fill ourselves up with enough love and attention and praise to somehow assuage our inner doubt and restlessness. Our habit leads us to avoid, or indulge, or subdue the various instincts—anything except letting them in.

Human Nature

Our anxious desires signal our need for care and attention. Imagine if someone stopped at your home, asking for a drink of water. You could think of how to get rid of them, you could hide under the bed and pretend not to be home, you could say you've somehow run out of water, you could throw things out the window at them to frighten them away. I know all that sounds mad, but that's exactly what we do when our instincts turn up. We do anything except let them in. But maybe you can simply open the door—listen to what they need, give them a moment's care and attention, and see how they respond.

We are constantly invited to come to the door of our experience. What does the restlessness or need feel like in your body? What does it want? How does it change if you make a little space for it? In the end, what you really want, no matter how intense or neurotic your reactions may be, is simply to be cared for and attended to.

REFLECTIVE INQUIRY

One way to do this is with the powerful reflective question: What do I *really* want? Whether a desire for security, intimacy, or approval: What do I *really* want? You might find many layers of responses. Let them move through and ask again: OK, and what do I *really* want? Writing can help to focus the reflection. Ask yourself the question and write whatever comes to mind. Don't censor yourself. Then: OK, and what do I *really* want?

The instincts appear, like much of our experience, in ways that are out of our control. We can decide very small things in life—whether to continue reading now or get a cup of tea, to eat this or that for lunch. But the vast majority of our experience is out of our control—what we think, how we feel, how long we live. Life happens by itself, flowing naturally out of limitless causes and conditions. We don't get to choose much of the content, but we can train ourselves in the art of responding to it.

We do not need to suppress our biology, and we cannot transcend it. But we can increasingly live fully and fluidly and freely within it.

This is the invitation of our practice.

4

The Psychological Body

Most of us are unconscious prisoners of our psychology.

We act out our patterning, instead of entering into and exploring it. Pulled and pushed around by our (usually unhelpful) self-talk, we constantly narrate, analyze, and judge our experience. When people first start meditating, they are often shocked by this inner commentary, and meditative awareness actually turns up the volume on the inner discourse, such that we start to see, maybe for the first time, just how shockingly self-involved we are.

There is a word the Buddha either used or made up: *ahamkara*. Literally, it means "*I*-making activity." If we want to invent a term, we could also call it "self-ing," the constant reinforcement of *me* and *my* at the heart of almost every thought. Most of our background mind-chatter seems to be just habitual blah-blah, but as you enter into your mind with awareness, you find that your inner narrative serves several powerful functions. It gives you your *self-image*, it acts repeatedly as *self-reinforcement*, and measures you by *self-judgment*.

We'll look now in detail at these primary ways we create, maintain, and act out our psychology.

SELF-IMAGE

How do you imagine yourself and describe yourself to yourself? How do you speak to yourself about yourself? Unless we wake up to our habitual narratives, they inevitably become self-fulfilling: you feel more and more like the person you tell yourself you are.

Our self-images are manifold. We base them partly on our physical attributes—age, sex, body shape and size, ethnicity, etc. We then add layers of historical material, built up from all the self-views that we first inherited, then internalized and concretized until they seem to be simply the truth about who and how we are. And then we filter these through our defensive and deficient feelings—we develop the armor of shame or arrogance around our innermost sense of self to defend ourselves against how we believe others perceive us.

Waking up to our psychology is a lifelong process. Meditation has helped me enormously to understand my own habits of mind, but so too have more explicitly psychological modes of inquiry.

Sometimes on retreats, I might ask people to spend some time exploring their self-views in pairs or small groups. Take some time now to do a similar exercise, in writing. Look at the seven contemplative questions below and write answers to each. Don't censor yourself. Don't look for a "correct" answer. Write down whatever comes to mind:

- How do you think of yourself?
- Which qualities get emphasized?
- Which others might you ignore or minimize?
- Do you have a mainly appreciative or mainly critical self-view?
- How do you feel about the size and shape of your body?
- Which three words would you use first to describe yourself?
- Complete this sentence ten times, without thinking too much. Just writing down the first thing that comes to mind: I'm someone who . . .

And now take a moment to reflect on your answers.
Read them back to yourself. Are there themes that emerge?

What flavor do your views have—are they fearful, critical, limiting, or are they encouraging and empowering?

Are they true?

Are they useful?

Are they kind?

An exercise like the one above is one way to explore and expose your various self-images (they are always plural—we think of ourselves as a coherent somebody, but we find many versions of ourselves, often in competition and conflict with each other). We invent, believe, and reinforce our self-views with little regard for reality.

THE SOCIAL SELF-IMAGE: WHO DOES SOCIETY SAY YOU ARE?

There are many aspects of self-image that are personal, but before exploring them, I first want to acknowledge some of the *socially constructed* aspects of self-image that we all inherit, and all too easily perpetuate.

In the questions I asked above, how much did identity signifiers like ethnicity, gender, and sexual orientation contribute to your self-image? The chances are that the more you belong to a socially dominant or majority identity, the less that part will stand out to you. For example, if you are white-skinned, I'd be surprised if *white* was one of the three words that immediately come to mind in identifying yourself. White-centric society (which inevitably means *white supremacist* society) implicitly reinforces white as normal, so it doesn't stand out to white people. Ethnicity or race is much more likely to figure in the self-image of those who are considered different from the norm—and minority groups have their difference or "otherness" constantly reinforced. Implicitly or explicitly, our cultural norms and biases reinforce certain messages that form not only our self-images, but also a sense of how acceptable or welcome that self is in different settings.

If you are a woman, you certainly know something about society suggesting to you a self-image of being lesser—one reinforced by wage gaps, abortion laws, taxes on feminine hygiene products, sexual victim-blaming, and many other examples from a long, depressing and all-too-familiar list. Nonwhites, especially (but not exclusively) those living in a majority white country, know this too, from constant exposure to unconscious bias, as well as to overt racism. And if you are nonheterosexual or noncisgender,* or hearing- or vision-impaired or mobility-challenged, or if you have an Islamic-sounding name and travel regularly through international airports, then likewise, you know something personally, and probably painfully, about discrimination and prejudice.

If on the other hand, you are a light-skinned, heterosexual, able-bodied, cisgender man (like the one writing this book), then whatever challenges and tragedies you may have traversed in your life, you have nevertheless grown up in and moved through a world that is pretty much optimized for your social identity. Which means inevitably that, unless you have given a lot of care and attention to recognizing and undoing your inevitable unconscious identity-blindness, you don't know much about how this stuff works.

This in turn is a big part of how dominance gets perpetuated: those benefiting from a dominant social identity tend to know very little about the experience of the minority groups, whereas those with a marginalized identity know a *lot* about the majority groups. That is why, when it comes to issues of racism, homophobia, and other social identity issues, dominant groups (hello, fellow white men) mostly need to do a lot of listening and not very much talking, at least at first. Which, of course, is exactly the opposite of what they are culturally conditioned to do.

People in majority categories, then, tend to be blind to the social components of their identity. (White people may just feel they live in a body. Black people know very well that theirs is a *black body*). Black people know very well how their blackness affects their self-image. Likewise for transgender people. But if you are white,

---

* If you don't know what this means, *please* learn about it.

and/or heterosexual, how does your whiteness, and/or your straight-ness, affect your self-image?

I would love to think that this book is being read by an all-inclusive great rainbow coalition of social identities. And I can well imagine that the majority of my readers is most likely white. If that's you, I'm not suggesting you have never been marginalized or dis-missed. I'm sure there have been times—in your family, at school, among peers—in which you have personally felt alone and excluded, different or wrong, unfairly treated or criticized. And you'll know that the emotional residue of these situations can last for decades, painfully impacting your self-image as someone who is different, or unworthy, or misunderstood. Perhaps then, you can imagine for a moment what your life would be like if that feeling of exclusion were being perpetuated by most of the powers, institutions, and attitudes that make up what we call "society."

While teaching in Paris recently, I was staying near a prestigious culinary school, which I passed on my way to and from the teaching venue. A row of eleven large photo boards showed young people in a variety of fine-dining and *hôtellerie* roles as part of a recruitment campaign for the school. And yes, all eleven students, plus everyone featured in the backgrounds, were white. What do those boards say to nonwhite Parisian youth? Basically: This is not for you, there is no one like you here, you are not represented and, therefore, not welcome.

Extracurricular Exercise for White People

Often, unfortunately, it is the same in meditation centers. Many times I've been shown a flier or a website or a brochure for a medita-tion course or center with no nonwhite representation. White read-ers, imagine for a moment if it were the other way around:

You've heard about a teacher or practice that speaks about train-ing your mind, freeing the heart, and developing compassion for all beings. You are instinctively drawn to their ideas and have been curious about meditation. You go to their website where the teacher and many students are pictured, looking healthy, peaceful, and happy.

Everyone pictured is black. Nobody looks like you.

How included do you feel?

The texts mention "all beings" but as far as you can see in all the images, no white beings are included. How invited would you feel to attend a class?

Tentative but still curious, you go along to the class. Arriving, you see all these black people arriving, chatting, welcoming each other. You perceive broad similarities in the kinds of clothes they wear, the social class they seem to belong to—the linguistic expressions they use—similarities that they all seem to share and to understand easily and instinctively, but which feel distant or unusual to you.

How welcome do you feel?

Some people seem a little uneasy about your presence. Some try to be friendly but seem anxious or clumsy around you. Nobody mentions anything explicit about you, but you feel different, the unwelcome "white sheep" of a meditation family, the glaring white elephant person in the room.

How likely are you to return?

Really doing the above exercise as a visualization may give a small taste of how people can be made to feel different, other, uncomfortable, unwelcome. This happens to all of us in different ways, but for some people social conditions reinforce this experience in countless ways throughout their lives. And our social conditioning plays a large part in constructing our psychological selves.

The bodies we live in can be included or excluded, approved or disapproved of, normalized or stigmatized, welcomed or rejected.

Body Image

Let's just spend a few moments with the words "my body."

My body.

Repeat that to yourself a few times and feel into whatever associations, images, and feelings arise. *My body.* What is that? Who is that? Do you like the associations that you notice? Is the impact broadly positive or negative? *My body.* This body you are sitting in right now, reading in, living in. When you contemplate it, does it seem basically lovable? Or unlovable?

There are all kinds of pressures around body image, cultural, familial, and personal layered one on top of another. This is true for everyone, but as we've seen above, the cultural pressures are different for different groups and are disproportionate in their impact. For example, for women there is the cultural reinforcement of a certain narrow body image—one that is often bound to an ideal of youthfulness and beauty, one that attempts to squeeze the variety of human body types into a particular cultural conformity.

Following is a series of contemplative questions, which may be more poignant for, and more often directed to, women. However, we can all reflect on them, wherever on the gender spectrum we identify:

What is your ideal body-image?

Where did that ideal come from?

How does the body you are in right now compare to it?

And: how do you respond to the previous questions? Do you find yourself (unwillingly perhaps), despite understanding the perniciousness of body-idealizing and shaming, nevertheless comparing yourself to some ideal, and subsequently telling yourself a story about how you are and how you should be? I remember a piece of good advice from the Sunscreen Song: "Don't read beauty magazines. They will only make you feel ugly."

What do I look like?

What do others think of how I look?

Should I look different from or "better" than this?

Would surgery help?

Is my nose/butt/thighs/belly/arms or anything else too big/small/narrow/wide/flabby/skinny or something else?

There is no way to win against the perniciousness of that inner pressure. But all the desires and attempts to look different are really wishes to *feel different* about ourselves. I saw a documentary once about teenage girls getting cosmetic surgery. One fifteen-year-old, flicking through a catalog of nose shapes, said, "People say I'm vain. But I just want to be happy." She turned back to the catalog as if it actually contained the source of happiness—as if those with ideal-shaped noses must be perfectly content, as if she, once graced with a slightly differently shaped olfactory organ, would be *happy*.

One of the most fundamental practices for living freely in our bodies is coming out of our ideas and images of the body, into the lived experience. This is the primary way we both wake up to our unconscious ideals and free ourselves from their pernicious influence.

From Pudgy to Prosperous

I grew up with asthma. It was serious enough that I had a few occasions, aged seven to fourteen, when I was hospitalized in a blue-light-siren-oxygen-mask kind of a way. I couldn't participate in sports at school—running fifty meters left me feeling panicked and sucking hard to get enough air into my lungs. It also left me feeling clumsy, fragile, and uneasy in my body. I felt "pudgy," a word that even as I write it now evokes whispered echoes of shame and self-hatred. Most of all, I thought I shouldn't be the way I was. When I look at photographs of me as a child, I'm sometimes still surprised to see that I don't actually look particularly "pudgy," but that was the self-view that I internalized. In my first few months in India I lost about eighteen kilograms (forty pounds) in weight—the sudden result of a diet without either meat or beer. I could see my ribs, but the inner feeling of being overweight, ungainly, and of "huffing and puffing" whenever I exerted myself persisted.

I started to actively investigate my body-image. I uncovered layers of shame about asthma, exacerbated by teasing at school and feeling excluded from sports teams. I saw how my relationship to my body was both distorted and out of date. At twenty years old, I still actually felt preadolescent. I began drawing crude self-portraits to see which elements I unconsciously emphasized or diminished. I saw how I would exaggerate the proportions of my arms and legs, leaving me with a shrunken chest and a collapsed belly, and realized that this is how I was living my life. My attention went to my arms and legs, investing in the limbs of action and movement, while ignoring the chest—center of breath and emotion—and the belly—center of being embodied and grounded. So I began to consciously sit and breathe and walk and sense and feel my way back into my torso. Back into my breathing chest and belly. Back into the aliveness of my emotional life. Back into the fullness of an embodied, em-bellied presence.

During several intense months of this, my asthma disappeared. After thirteen years of never ever being without a steroidal inhaler, I put my last one on a shrine in Thailand that had been set up for recovering addicts to leave their opium pipes and walked away. My chest had come to know an inner feeling of space and openness and ease that was hitherto unimaginable. I began to experience my belly as a warm, easy sense of home—rounded and relaxed. I felt like one of those big-bellied buddhas, whose images express a full-belliedness that symbolizes the kind of ease and contentment one knows after a satisfying meal—expansive, satiated, content, and prosperous. Regardless of your physical size or weight, having a relaxed, round belly feels very gratifying.

My practice took me from feeling pudgy to feeling potbellied, in the most surprising and nourishing way.

MIND THE GAP

From a purely aesthetic point of view, my
body was better when I was twenty-two. But
I didn't enjoy it. I was too busy comparing it
to everybody else's.

—CINDY CRAWFORD

Maybe you have had that experience of looking at a photograph of yourself taken ten, twenty, or thirty years ago. You marvel at the youth and beauty and vitality that shine out of you in those earlier years. Yet simultaneously, you remember how insecure or dissatisfied you were with your body at the time. Is the same true right now? Are you overly concerned about the body you are living with today, which in another ten years you might look back on and love? Aging is a one-way street—which means that this moment right now is the most youthful you'll ever be! It's an invitation to enjoy the remarkable body you have right now. Whatever your current condition of health or sickness or injury, here is a feeling, sensing, living organism—and the vitality and energy that animate it. Appreciate it as it is, especially as you don't know how long it will last.

This is an example of how we view ourselves through a dysmorphic lens—a perception gap between how we actually are and how we perceive and describe ourselves. How you experience your body usually tells you more about your psychology than your physicality. Like a hall of mirrors, we distort our sense of size, shape, or perceived attractiveness. We obsess over some aspect of our physical appearance. We look at that photograph and construct an idealized past body—we agonize over diets or exercise and plan for an idealized future body—and all the while, we either ignore or disassociate from or criticize our present body—the living, breathing one sitting here, taking in experience right now.

To close that gap, we practice returning to our *immediate* body—one that is not imagined or described, but which is *felt* from the inside. We do this by inhabiting and reinhabiting the breathing process—the sensations of this bodily moment—by feeling into the habitual tension patterns that we might find in our jaw or shoulders or belly. Feel for yourself a moment, right now. Is your jaw a little tight? Are your shoulders a little hunched? Is your breathing relaxed or somewhat constrained? If so, and if you relax a little, feel if that allows for a more easeful presence as you sit here, reading. What might it be like to be more or less constantly attuned to this present body, to the felt sense of inhabiting life, right here?

Orienting in this way to our "present body," we recover a body we can live in *as it is* rather than how we imagine or describe it. And like this, we begin to recognize and explore the distortions in our body-image.

Now we'll explore how some of those distortions function, and then look at how they can be opened, understood, and resolved.

THE AGE GAP

How old would you be if you didn't know
how old you are?

—SATCHEL PAIGE

Many of us live with an inner age gap, which has several versions. The first is the feeling of being younger than our years. A certain youthful enthusiasm and vitality tell me I am not really old, I've just been young for a *really* long time now. Then the mirror shocks me as I walk past, suddenly confronted by one who looks so much older than I feel. This gap is quite understandable: The *inmost feeling of me* seems immutable, ageless. I intuit an essential *me-ness* that doesn't change or dim—that orbits around the same basic concerns and wishes as it ever has, at least since early adulthood. Memory links this inner self-sense all the way back to when I first recognized myself as "adult" and tells me I still feel the same.

Research, by the way, apparently has shown that this kind of lower "subjective age" correlates with a healthier brain, fewer age-related impairments, and a better sex life, so there is definitely something to be said for being "young at heart." Others experience the gap in the other direction, appearing "old before their time." They may seem to age psychologically ahead of their physical years, and adopt clothing, activities, and attitudes that they hope will somehow help them arrive at that mysterious life-station called "grown-up." An inner concern about not really feeling adult often leads to this as a compensation, yet the inner experience easily remains one of feeling somehow young, inadequate, or small.

But the age gap often feels more anxious and insecure than that. Internet forums like Quora or Ask Google are full of people expressing doubt and concern about their subjective age gap. Recent examples at the time of writing include:

"I am in my twenties but still feel like a teenager."

"I'm in my thirties—when will I feel like a grown-up?"

"I recently turned forty but still feel like a twenty-five-year-old."

Behind this discrepancy is the confusion of feeling dystonic, where perception and reality are clearly out of sync. People also speak about "coming to terms with" turning thirty, forty, fifty, sixty. We'll look in a later chapter at our relationship to mortality and the inevitability of aging, but first let's explore more the anxiety of being a biological adult yet psychologically feeling like a child.

THE DEFICIENT AGE GAP

While our biological age is measured in years, our *felt age* can vary from moment to moment, mostly depending on how *comfortable, confident, and capable* we feel in different situations. The more at ease one is, the more adult one feels, and the more deficient one believes oneself to be, the more childlike or small one feels. By being present with the shifts in our felt age we find the deficient age gaps in our psyche.

I used to feel insecure in social situations. I would start to feel uncomfortable during a conversation, wondering what the person might be thinking of me. Was I being clear enough? Smart enough? Witty enough? And though my visual perception didn't change, the other person would start quite literally to seem larger, more authoritative, and important, while I began to feel smaller, less empowered, and younger.

This young feeling is very important to recognize. It shows us where we don't feel "grown-up," where part of us still feels small and deficient. Consider for yourself for a moment: Where in your life do you really feel like an adult? And in what situations or relationships do you feel young, small, insecure?

Adultness feels confident, capable, comfortable. There is a sense of ease. You trust yourself. Doubt and anxiety either don't arise or are merely peripheral. Maybe you can find certain areas of your life where this kind of adult relationship to experience is very clear. It may be with regard to a specific skill you have developed, something you know you are good at. It may be available in certain relationships, where you know that your knowledge is respected or your authority and boundary setting are clear and appropriate. Recognizing and familiarizing yourself with the inner feeling of this adult sense, wherever you have access to it, is an important way of tasting and trusting your psychological maturity.

There may be other areas in which you either already know or as you explore this you can find out that you feel distinctly *un*-adult—situations where you feel small, young, insecure. For some people this is an almost all-pervading condition, especially when difficult childhood circumstances have not really been addressed or resolved. For others, it may feel like being out of one's depth, arising in certain situations. You know you are caught in a deficient age gap when you feel helpless—anxious, afraid of criticism, fraudulent, self-conscious. As well as your mental narrative telling you about your deficiency, if you feel into the *felt-sense* of your experience—the inner sense of identity in that moment—you will discover that you perceive yourself as small, young, childlike, helpless.

It can be profoundly uncomfortable to stay present within this, because we have been conditioned to think we *should be* adults. Our peers look as if they are adults, so we pretend that we are too, not realizing that they may be as busy as we are trying to look confident and competent, while feeling anything but.

This is the territory of what is sometimes called the inner child. A deficient sense of self trying to feel sufficient—not knowing how to be oneself, yet imagining everyone else knows how. As R. D. Laing expressed this confusion:

I feel you know what I'm supposed to know
but you can't tell me what it is
because you don't know
that I don't know what it is.

WAKING UP, GROWING UP, SHOWING UP

We carry the legacy of our childhood development within us. Contacting, befriending, and exploring this is part of how we both *wake up* to our psychology and *grow up* into psychological maturity.

If I refer to your *psyche*, you might think of your mind. But as we can see from the examples in this chapter, tracking your *embodied, physical* experience is vitally important in accessing your *psyche*, in exploring and transforming your psychological material.

Psychological transformation is about *growing up* internally. As I recognize the areas where I feel inwardly young, I can meet and metabolize those places which got shut down or frozen early on in life. We find clear correlations between our deficient states and the events in our early lives that formed them.

Spiritual work is often spoken about in terms of *waking up*— seeing through our defenses and delusions to a clearer sense of reality. This clear seeing can dissolve our patterning in the immediacy of the seeing, but the patterns are *dissolved* in the moment, rather than fully *resolved*. Waking up to a clearer seeing is different from doing the inner work to meet, explore, and digest our psychological patterning. And both are necessary if we want to see clearly and act freely.

These two dimensions of inner work are equally important. The first few years of my own practice were all about the waking up. I was spending a lot of time in intensive meditation retreats, and my practice was clearly and intently focused on a vision of liberation, *beyond* the realm of *I*, *me*, and *my*. Rather than entering into and exploring my inner stories and their effects on me, I was instead trying to just see past them, push through them, get them out of the way. I was trying to avoid my own psychology, trying to not get caught up in the messy world of *self*. I had after all spent the first couple of decades of my life doing just that, and Buddhism seemed to be say-ing, "Hey, all that self-ing is the problem. Give it up, go beyond it, and you will emerge into the open field of freeness, out beyond the petty world of *me*."

That was so appealing, because my own *me-world* was full of anxiety and insecurity. I would worry about what I wanted. I would worry about what I thought. I would worry about what oth-ers thought about me and about what they thought about what I thought. The only inner resources I had were my thoughts, and they were just mind-spaghetti, tangled in a labyrinth of confusion.

So when I discovered meditation, I was really motivated to "get out of my head," to unhook my attention from my thoughts and see clearly beyond my mind. I learned to recognize abstrac-tion and drop it. I learned to stay present as the knowing-mind: aware, steady, imperturbable. In this clarity, the light of awareness seemed to dazzle my habitual thoughts. They would wither in the glare, and I would find myself open to experience without any cen-tral reference point. Thought would give way to a wide-open field of awareness, luminous and all-encompassing. I would sit in my hut listening to the crow calls in the cedar trees outside and know no separation from them. I was the bird, and its call, and the sky it flew across. I was the tree it sat in, the wind that blew through its leaves, and the knowing of it all, simultaneously. I was free of my self-imprisonment in the anxious, doubtful, compulsive world of *me*.

And then the bell would ring. And I would uncross my sore legs and sit and drink chai overlooking the valley below me, watch-ing the woodsmoke curl up through those same cedar trees. And I would still feel a certain contemplative intimacy with it all. Yet with-out the formality of meditation practice, as I sat and watched and drank and listened, *usual-mind* would start to reassert itself. And the same old patterns of mind would be back. During meditation they had *dissolved*, but evidently had not been *resolved*, because here they were again.

In those days I was quite terrified of people. Intense meditation experiences had left me feeling wide open in a way that was profoundly liberating, yet also left me quite unable to function normally. When I met people, I didn't know what to do; I seemed to have lost my sense of social cues and interactions and would become gripped by fear, often quite intensely. Every few days I would set off early to walk the several kilometers into the nearest town to buy vegetables, hoping to arrive, make my purchases, and leave again before seeing anyone else. I was quite comfortable with the local Indian and Tibetan people but extremely uncomfortable with the foreigners who lived in the surrounding hills, many of them there to be close to the Dalai Lama or other Tibetan monasteries and masters.

Walking through the forest paths on the way to or from the market, I would see a *videshi* (foreigner) approaching in the distance and my mind would begin racing: *What shall I do? Should I say hello? Smile? Put my hands together in silent greeting? Or keep my eyes down and pass silently?* This torturous inner dialogue would intensify as the person approached, and I would then do any one of the above, somewhat awkwardly, as they passed. Then the doubt would start up again: *Why did I do X? What did they think? Why didn't I do Y instead?* This would be compounded by what in the Buddhist tradition is called the "second arrow" of suffering—the additional layer we add to our initial discomfort—in this case doubting the doubt, judging the judgment: *What's the matter with me? Why can't I just greet someone normally? I shouldn't be so complicated about it. I have to stop doing this. I'm so clumsy around people.* And then, a third arrow for good measure: *I'm supposed to be mindful! I should be feeling my feet on the ground, not worrying about how I do or don't say hello to people. I'm such a terrible practitioner. How will my practice ever progress?*

And all the while, underneath the painful inner doubt and criticism, was an inner young one, fearful of rejection—a sense of self that was small, afraid, and confused. This is how a deficient subjective age gap works. In moments when you feel insecure, afraid, frozen, or overwhelmed, you will usually find underneath a sense of being small, helplessness, young. And what that psychological structure needs—what it didn't get enough of at the time and is still hoping for—is to be met, welcomed, loved. It needs listening to, feeling into, staying open to. All the inner dialogue, so circular and self-critical, can do nothing to resolve it, because it is just fear meeting fear, criticism meeting criticism. And as Einstein says: "No problem can be solved on the same level of consciousness that created it."

This is not just about "being with" the experience, as the meditation literature endlessly encourages. It certainly includes basic mindful attention, or *being present inside* the felt experience. Yet it also has to include a certain openness to the background material—whatever associations, images, memories, or secondary feelings may arise. This is how we discern between the psychological imprints of past experience and the actual reality of present experience—when we address the imprints of the past through feeling and caring for the emotional residue. That is how the past gets, finally, digested and resolved.

I was pretty slow to deal with the past imprint of my insecurity around people and in many ways it took a certain quirk of fate or divine intervention or dumb luck or blessing of my teacher (pick one according to your personal belief system) for that to happen.

COMING DOWN FROM THE MOUNTAIN

About eighteen months into that first trip to India and Thailand, my teacher started to encourage me to go to England. He knew my parents were worried about me. This was 1991—pre-Internet. A letter took a week or two, and phone calls were unreliable and extremely expensive. I wrote to my parents regularly, but not of anything they could understand or wanted to hear. I wrote philosophical musings on the Buddha's teachings, on the nature of Mind and the state of the world, and many pages on what I thought was wrong with "Western Society." And my parents thought I was losing my mind (er, kind of) and falling under the influence of some strange, dangerous cult—conclusions that were perfectly reasonable, given the evidence. In addition, I had decided at some point to send them a photograph, hoping it would reassure them that I was happy and healthy. I didn't take into consideration that my hair had grown to my waist, that I'd lost eighteen kilograms in weight since they had seen me, and that sitting in full-lotus wearing a cotton *lunghi* wasn't how they were used to seeing me.

So Babaji told me to go home. Go and see my parents. Reassure them I was OK—and then if I wanted to, I could get some work, save some money, and come back to India. Given my general paranoia about speaking with people, this was an incredibly uncomfortable scenario. But I trusted my teacher and knew he was right, so I bought a ticket for London.

I left the ashram on March 15, 1991, wearing my *lunghi* and an orange turban around my long, matted hair. My luggage was a restitched rice sack, containing some *chimta* fire-tongs, an iron *tawa* for making chapati bread, and a few other items utterly unsuited to English life. I sat on the night bus to Delhi behind two English men with London accents who laughed and joked together—and I wondered how they did it.

The bus stopped for chai at dawn, before we hit the Delhi traffic. Babaji had packed *parathas* and *achaar* for me, which I took from my rice-bag, clanking the tongs and chapati plate together. The jokey Londoners, Frank and Brian, watched me in some bewilderment, until one asked, "What have you got in there, then?"

I began to talk (tentatively), explaining how sadhus tend their fires and how I had been living in some kind of "yogic seclusion" for the last many months. My insecurity told me they listened somewhat skeptically, but as we boarded the bus again, Frank gave me his card: "If you want a job, call me when you get to London." They owned Indian clothing and jewelery stalls in London markets, and once I returned to London, I began working for them in markets in Camden, Portobello Road, and St Martin's courtyard behind Trafalgar Square.

It was just what I needed. I started to relearn how to be with people—how to stay present in my experience, tracking whatever was happening in my mind and body, while also speaking, listening, responding. It was just as important an aspect of my meditation practice as those months in the mountains had been.

And it gave me an opportunity to really meet that little one. Being constantly exposed to people at the markets, I made a practice of tracking my insecurities—the ideas that people might not like me, the concern for how I was being perceived, the secret, shameful, almost desperate hunger for approval and love that was lurking beneath almost every interaction.

In this way, I started to give my inner child the unconditional care, acceptance, and attention that it had spent the last two decades crying out for. The attention of others will never quite do it. Though we can know moments of great love and tenderness from others, the only way we really satisfy our insecure needs is through providing that care and attention ourselves. Attending to the inner age gaps that we find—feeling into whatever sense of deficiency is inside them.

With an inner self-image so completely out of sync with reality, I kept on losing my adultness, feeling small every time insecurity arose—yet right there is also where I recovered it. Because it feels deficient, we want to turn away from it. It is counterintuitive to turn toward our pain, but doing so is at the very heart of true transformation. In turning *toward* your doubt and fear, your adult capacity can hold or parent your deficient feeling. Or, seen from a deeper perspective, we find that awareness can be the true parent to all experience.

This parenting is innate. By its very nature awareness is receptive, loving, always available to what arises. Right now, the experience of reading these words is appearing to you in awareness. Awareness doesn't withhold its attention from anything. It receives what appears, effortlessly, and endlessly makes room for all experience. Seen like this, we find that awareness *is* unconditionally loving. Accepting. Inclusive. And as we understand that, we find we can make room for *whatever* appears in consciousness—we find that all experience is welcome. Received in awareness, any and all experience can appear, have its expression, and fade. There is *no wrong experience*, nothing unworthy of care and attention, no thought that cannot be allowed—whatever its content. No feeling that cannot be welcomed, however deficient it may feel.

Awareness is the wide-open embrace in which all experience longs to be both held and released.

GOING BEYOND SELF-IMAGE

We can see how our self-images are psychological—yet they are held bodily as tension patterns and unconscious posturing. We explore them through our beliefs, our history, and the associated images and ideas we have, but we really meet and work with them in how they show up somatically. Bodily life is where our patterning is held and felt, and it is here too where it can be met and released.

A deficient sense of self can arise in many different ways, not only in relation to the age gap we just discussed. Another sense of deficiency easily arises around our sense of capacity. Our historical experiences may in various ways have dented our confidence, our basic trust in ourselves. When faced with something challenging then, the habitual response is "I can't," "I couldn't," or "What if I don't manage?" Fear of failure, unwillingness to try something new, resistance to leaving the familiar and the comfortable—these positions all arise from a painful sense of deficiency, our basic trust in self-images holding us back from growing our capacities.

I wanted to give people a chance to work with this on the Dharma Yatra, a project we began in 2001. On the *yatra* (the Sanskrit word for "pilgrimage"), up to two hundred people walked single file through Southern France, in silence, for six to eight hours per day, camping and exploring meditation and Dharma teachings along the way. We had a crèche vehicle for the children and a support truck that carried the luggage and tents and served as the mobile kitchen. Each night we'd build a whole tent village—and the kitchen would prepare dinner for two hundred. It was a feat to get two hundred people to wake in the morning, meditate, bathe, have breakfast, pack down their tents, stow their luggage, and be standing in a circle ready to leave by 9 a.m. I've gone camping in a group of four and we've struggled to get that together. The whole thing ran on *dana*, donations freely given—and not wanting to put the work burden on any one group, I made a rotating system for the four-person volunteer kitchen team. First day you would be "potato peeler," getting to know the ropes. Second day you would be "kitchen assistant." Third day you were sous-chef. Fourth day you would be head chef, planning the menu, buying the ingredients, directing the three other members of the kitchen team, and delivering the meal. Fifth day, you'd be back on the walk again.

If feeding two hundred people from the back of a truck sounds daunting, then you'd share that sentiment with pretty much everyone who was on the walk. We struggled to find kitchen team volunteers because people's self-image didn't include being a back-of-a-lorry mass caterer: "I can't do that. I've never cooked for that many. That would be too much for me." In the evening teachings, I spoke about our sense of self as deficient; the defeatist narratives we tell ourselves about how we are, what we can and cannot do, ways in which we might fail. It is reasonable, wise even, to be a little daunted by something new—but there is a big difference between wise caution and defeatist rhetoric. As we encouraged and supported people to join the kitchen it was beautiful to see what happened. The four days became an initiation of sorts and a way of exposing, and exploding, people's self-images. Fear and disbelief gave way to confidence and empowerment.

One person in particular enjoyed cooking but was extremely nervous about the scale of operation. All kinds of self-views jostled for attention, giving her ideas for why she wasn't up to it or might fail. I spoke to her on her fourth day as she stood overseeing the serving of her rice and dhal, curries and salad—towel tucked in her chef's apron and ladle in hand. She was glowing, partly no doubt with the heat in the back of the truck, but also with the liberation from her limiting view. She had met her fear and resistance, had persevered in the face of feeling inadequate or insecure, and seen that she could be someone other than the view she had of herself.

How do you meet a new challenge?

Do you recognize the sense of doubt and deflation that shows this limiting sense of self? How does it show up in your body? What might happen if you stood differently? If you opened your chest? If you listened not to the old ideas, but to the energy in your hands and arms, to the sturdiness of your feet on the ground?

"I Can Do Anything": The Counterphobic Self

For others, the self-image is shored up by a more counterphobic response. I have a dear friend whose response to pretty much any challenge at all is *Yes! Let's go.* It can feel very energizing to be around his enthusiasm and positivity, but shoring up one's self-image in this way can also be exhausting. Underneath the enthusiasm, there is actually desperation. Beneath the bravado, insecurity. The secret hope is that one will somehow prove to oneself by repeated attempts that one is OK. If I can beat my fear, if I can accomplish *X, Y,* and *Z,* then I'll be OK. If I can prove to everyone how capable I am, then I'll somehow believe it myself. If I can get rich enough, or clever enough, or skilled enough. If I can accumulate enough experiences or sleep with enough people or collect enough awards ... then I'll relax ... Then I'll be at peace ... Then I'll be OK ...

If you are one who tries to build and maintain a self-image in this way, it can be shocking and painful to recognize how much energy goes into that, and to feel the hollowness or fear beneath the confident exterior.

Please see for yourself for a moment. What kinds of self-image do you invest in? Is your basic orientation one of self-denigration or self-aggrandizement? When you see yourself in a mirror, how do you feel?

If you think someone is talking about you, what do you assume they might be saying?

This last question in particular might show you not only what assumptions you habitually make about yourself, but about how you expect others to confirm it, filling in your self-images with projections onto what others are thinking. How much freer and more fluid might your experience be, if you no longer believed in who you think you are?

Neither Edge nor Center

Insight meditation is explicitly designed to expose (and explode!) our habitual self-images, challenging them directly, experientially, and fundamentally, even, for example, in the very basic practice of giving mindful attention to this breathing body.

At first we have the impression that the body is an object—these three cubic feet (as songwriter Rufus Wainwright says) of bone and flesh—in which we place our meditative attention. This body has a shape, a gender, an age. These are my hands, these are my feet—this is my breath. But as our sensitivity grows, this sense of the body softens. The hard edges of the body stand out less. Attending to the sensations of bodily life directly, moment by moment, we don't find hands and feet or even inside and outside. We cannot really find where our folded legs end and the cushion—the world—begins. Our self-image idea will tell us, but our direct experience neither knows nor cares. Instead it settles into an intimacy with experience where body and world meet. Where sensation dances. Where we no longer mark where the sound of birdsong ends and the hearing of it begins. The body feels fluid and alive. Sensitive. Intimate with all experience. Truly sentient.

Try this again, similarly to how we did in a previous chapter, and right now, while you are here reading, tense your arms and legs and belly. Hold it a few moments and notice the density in your sensations. Feel how solid and real the boundary between inner and outer seems, and how strong the sense of being a self is.

And now . . . relax. Let go of that tension—allow your muscles to soften, breathe out, and notice how the sense of boundary also relaxes. Feel how the sense of self becomes more diffuse, the edges less defined.

This is just the gross layer of muscular relaxation. Most people are carrying all kinds of other tension patterns of which they are not even aware, as they are so habitually ingrained. Meditation teaches us to settle more and more deeply into our direct bodily experience, where the body as object gives way to an ever-changing dynamic flow of sensation and vibration, a constant streaming of felt experience through awareness. Present within this fluid bodily dance, we notice subtler layers of tension, numbness, and resistance and in turn give them the opportunity to move, open up, and soften. Then, however deeply we go into a particular sensation, we find no center. And however much we sense outward through the layers of sensation, we find no edge.

This profoundly affects our sense of what the body is and of how to inhabit it. Even when the experience isn't as tangible as described above, we begin to recognize the body as having neither edge nor center—as being a vast theater of experience, sensitive and responsive. Becoming familiar with this dimension, we see how our psychological patterning informs our tension patterns, and these too begin to open up. We discover a natural ease that underpins physical existence, the more our physical defenses and imagined deficiencies get resolved.

In the process of the body opening up in this way, it is common to have various kinds of nonordinary bodily perceptions, especially during meditation practice. These can show up as extremes of temperature or density or size. One might feel as if one's body is expanding hugely—as if the room cannot contain your physical form. The impression can be so strong that you are tempted to open your eyes and check! It equally can happen in the other direction, feeling as if the body is shrinking . . . vanishing even. Changes in the density of sensation can make you feel as if the body is becoming extremely light. If you open your eyes at this moment, you may be disappointed to find you're not actually levitating, though it can feel very much that way. Or the opposite can happen, in which the body feels incredibly dense, and the idea of moving even a finger seems like it would both take colossal effort and cause ripples throughout the universe.

It can feel as if your nervous system is reconfiguring itself, and in many ways that is exactly what is happening. Patterning that has been held rigidly, perhaps for decades, is starting to open up, and it is this energetic unwinding that causes the unusual perceptions, which can also include swaying or shaking, or occasional sudden spasms of movement.

These experiences are a natural part of an evolving capacity to inhabit this body more fully and freely. They are not particularly significant in themselves. Some find them exhilarating, exciting— others find them a little frightening and disorienting. What's significant is the insight—knowing the body can appear in many different ways, so that the usual psychological identification with our various self-images as being *who I am* just seems more and more limited, narrow, false, and unnecessary.

Increasingly, our reliance on self-images thins out and can completely disappear. Notice I didn't say the images themselves, but *the reliance on them*. You will still show up in the world *as if* you are this body, or as if it is yours, but it is no longer a source of seeming truth for the sense of *who I am*. You might go to the doctor for a pain in your arm, but even while explaining it and rolling up your sleeve to be examined, a freer relationship is clear to you. There is a close, caring relationship to this physicality, but without ownership and identification. We'll come back to this more in a later chapter.

Ultimately, all our self-images are partial at best—caricatures of how we imagine and describe ourselves, distorted in the hall of mirrors of the self describing the self to the self. We investigate these self-images in order to understand them and see through them, for that which you become familiar with no longer fools you—that which you see through becomes transparent.

SELF-IDENTITY

We've seen how we create ideas and images of who we are, then find ourselves trapped within them. Another aspect of how our psychological self gets maintained and acted out is through self-reinforcement, or *self-identity*.

Much of our habitual thought loops endlessly around the same old territory. We repeatedly go over what has happened previously, we idly imagine what might happen next, and we vaguely narrate to ourselves what is happening now. Depressingly little of our thinking is genuinely original or inspiring, and all of that habitual mind-noise is playing in our psyche like a local radio station left on in the background, often so consistently and monotonously that we barely notice it.

But when we start to practice meditation, we really begin to notice—especially if you do a meditation retreat, which is like turning the volume up, increasing your sensitivity to just how much of that background noise is really going on most of the time. Initially this cluttered thought just seems like a lot of hot air, endless blah-blah, mostly devoid of clarity or usefulness, boringly repetitive in its subject matter, and largely unnoticed except for in quiet moments like when you are trying to get to sleep and your inner radio station DJ just won't shut up.

REFERENCE POINTS FOR REALITY

Actually though, that habitual, low-level inner chat is doing much more than just cluttering the airwaves of your mind. It is constantly reinforcing an inner network of reference points, which become the arbiters for what we take to be reality:

I like A.

I wonder about B.

C happened so quickly.

I remember D.

I would really like to go to E.

It is going to be too late for F.

Shouldn't things be more G?

H would be hilarious.

I can't believe J would do that.

K is taking a long time.

L was really fun.

Why can't M be different?

What would happen if I were N?

That reminds me of O.

P makes me really uncomfortable.

Q is so interesting.

I don't understand R.

Etc., etc.

This is how that habitual thought plays out. It roams around the three fields of time, repeatedly referencing and reinforcing (and therefore *identifying with*) a sense of past, present, and future. It goes back and forth, establishing networks of time and place, inner and outer, self and other, before and after, right and wrong.

It is so familiar we don't notice it. But when we really attend, we notice the primary nodes on this constantly reinforced network: *space—time—self—world*. These reference points are so familiar, so universally agreed and reinforced in all our interactions, that they seem, well, real. So what would happen if we just stopped reinforcing them for a while? If we allowed the mind to give them up, to let them go and float awhile, untethered by these reference points?

I know, it's not so easy. That's the nature of habits—we keep on doing it. So at first, we take up the practice of intentionally leaving those thoughts alone. Again and again and again. Just unhooking. Unmooring awareness from the anchor of thinking. Dropping that thought. And this one. And this one. Over and over and over. Do this sincerely and steadily for a while—through formal meditation practice, but also in any and every moment you remember throughout the day—and you start to notice the gaps between thoughts. And in this space, there is possibility.

Around each thought, prior to it, and remaining after it, we find an open, spacious, *knowing quality*, which we call awareness—the space in which the thoughts arise.

Usually, we identify with our thinking. The *I* thought arises and we take it to be who we are: *I am writing these words*, for example. Or in your case, *I am reading these words*. This is so normal sounding as to appear obvious, and mostly we cannot even see any other possibility, so it goes unquestioned. But if you are indeed the one who thinks that thought, then how come you can also *notice* the thought? If you are the one who is thinking, *who is the one who is noticing?*

Now we are really in the territory of meditation, where we need a different way, a *nonconceptual* way to meet experience. Because here, clearly, rational mind cannot help us. It will do you no good to simply think about thinking! All the while you are fully identified with your thinking—and for most people that means basically their entire lives—the usual sense of reality is getting constantly reinforced. *Every thought* does it. Try thinking a thought that does not reference self or other, time or space! Meditation, then, is the process by which we make the shift from identifying with our thinking to noticing our thinking. It teaches you that *you are not your thoughts.*

The Matrix

Who or what, then, is doing the noticing? We'll return to this in a later chapter.

First, let's explore this stepping back from thought-identification and the effect of that shift on what we could call (because it sounds cool, but is actually also quite an accurate description), our *time-space-self-other reality matrix.*

In Buddhism, Indra's net is a model representing the constructed fabric of reality—a consciousness-spanning infinitely jeweled matrix where each node is a jewel, reflecting all other nodes, interconnected like threads in a net. And each thought—every idea, image, and impulse—does the connecting, with our attention bouncing between points, constructing and reinforcing the reality net. This thought-net gives us a coherent sense of reality, where *self* is recognizable, *others* are familiar, *space* is measured, and *time* passes.

Self is the primary reference, of course. Almost every single thought concerns oneself in some way. *Other* is the counterpoint, a dichotomic reference by which I recognize and contrast myself. I am here, you are there. I am like this, and you, or they, are like that.

If *self* is the starring role and *other* the supporting actor, please meet some more of the cast: *memory* (the sense of past) keeps these nodes accessible, drawing on all our prior perceptions, wearing the costume of either nostalgia (pleasant) or regret (unpleasant). *Imagination* (the sense of future) creates connections like a spider spinning webs between points, dressing up in either the positively charged clothes of hope and fantasy or negatively charged ones of fear and anxiety. Then *description and analysis* (the sense of presence) get the scriptwriting credit, narrating experience as it unfolds.

Between thoughts of self and other/world and thoughts concerning past, present, and future, the net is complete. And you are caught in it. You are, as the old London expression goes, "Done up like a kipper" in the net of the time-space-self-world reality matrix.

Time, then, to take the red pill. To see through the matrix of self-reinforcement we give ourselves the opportunity, and the skill (called *practice*), to free ourselves from the net. To look past our thoughts. When we disidentify from our thinking, even momentarily, then that space opens up. It has to. Infinite conscious knowing (awareness) is the space wherein the matrix hangs—the endless empty limitless sky across which the jeweled net of Indra is suspended.

Unhook from habitual thoughts and you cannot help but feel into this space. This is how we find our way from the thinking to the noticing—from being caught in the net of thought content to exploring the space of thought-awareness. Suddenly you are no longer telling yourself the familiar stories about self and other, time and space. The net dissolves and reality opens up.

This experience may be familiar to you in various ways—from moments in meditation maybe, or through experiments with psychedelics, or in times of being struck by great beauty—looking up at the jeweled net of the starry night sky or gazing at the vastness of the ocean. In situations like these, thought occasionally surrenders itself briefly—life suddenly reveals itself as vast, mysterious, and irreducible to conceptual understanding.

There is a way right now, within the simple immediacy of sitting here, that we might incline our minds in that direction:

The Universe at the End of the Breath

Try this:

Tune in for a moment to the simple felt sense of sitting here. Feel the weight of the body sitting—the pressure of contact with chair or the ground.

Feel the natural immediacy of being here. The body is alive. Mind is awake. Life is happening. Experience is flowing through awareness.

Feel into the rhythm and movement of your breathing. Feel the natural expansion that happens through the in-breath . . . the natural relaxation that expresses through the out-breath . . . the momentary still point that is there between breaths.

Really let your attention settle into these three qualities: the natural expansion that happens when breathing in—the natural relaxation of breathing out—the natural stilling and stopping between breaths.

Give particular attention to that momentary stillness after the out-breath, however brief it may be, every time it comes around. At the end of the out-breath is a kind of energetic stopping. Feel into it, with the intention in that moment of pause to let everything come to rest. To let everything . . . STOP.

Allow the next in-breath to come by itself. Every time you come to the end of the out-breath, let your belly be soft. Let your attention drop down, down, down into your belly. Feel the texture of this rounded belly wherein breath and movement has stopped.

There may be a quality of emptiness or fullness, darkness or light. Notice whatever texture is present and allow the stopped-ness. See if this physical stopping has an effect on thinking. Let your thoughts dissolve into the relaxation of the out-breath, disappearing completely in that moment of stillness.

Keep sitting in this way, allowing a natural rhythm of breathing and directing your attention particularly down into your lower belly—

Down into the empty space between breaths

Down into the stilling of thought

Down into the depths of awareness

Down into the empty space which contains both sensation and thought, yet remains untouched by them

Down with each out-breath

Down past the breath, into stillness

Down here

Down into the body of your psychology

The body of your experience

The body of existence.

THE PAIN OF HOLDING ON

Letting go is a practice. Meditation teaches us to drop our thoughts patiently and persistently, relentlessly and repeatedly. And we do it, because we see the possibility of that open space—of *freedom from thinking* instead of carrying the same old views and beliefs and desires around with us, weighing us down.

Maybe you know that story of the two Zen monks crossing a river. Arriving at a river crossing they meet a woman who can't manage the swift current, and one of the monks helps the woman by carrying her across. The two monks continue on their way, but the second monk is giving off the sort of silent vibes you get when someone is full of indignation and outrage and trying to hide it. Finally, he can no longer contain himself: "What were you doing back there? How could you pick up that woman? You know it's against our training precepts to even touch a woman!" The first monk responds with a lightness of touch: "Yes," he says, "but I put her down afterward. You're still carrying her."

Habitual thought, then, needs to be gently put down. Over and over, *bazillions* of times, and then some more. But there's more to our psychological reinforcement than just those dull old background thoughts. There's also the reinforcement that's really psychologically hardwired—the core beliefs that have been going on so long—reinforced since early childhood (at least). This longest-serving, early psychological material is much harder to recognize as mere self-reinforcement, because it presents really compellingly as being *who I am—who I've always been—who I will always be.*

"That's the way I am," we say with a shrug, as if that is something immutable.

But it's not!

We can utterly, unimaginably transform our experience of ourselves, and our way of meeting life.

Dissolving and Resolving

Meditation teachings can sometimes aim too quickly beyond the psychological realm. Reaching for the open space beyond, we end up literally "overlooking" our psychological content, a phenomenon sometimes called *spiritual bypassing.* Somebody may have learned to dissolve a sticky or problematic thought, seeing through it to the open space beyond, yet the pattern isn't undone. It hasn't been understood. It is momentarily *dissolved,* but it hasn't been *resolved.* So the more intense material—the oldest and therefore most reinforced psychological patterning—inevitably keeps circling back around, unresolved, destined to repeat history because it is still hoping for care and attention. Indeed, these patterns usually got formed precisely because of a situation where we didn't get enough care and attention. If when they appear, we simply drop them, or *dissolve them into awareness,* then they still don't get that care and attention. So whereas the general blah-blah of our monkey-minds can just be left alone and unhooked from, the more impactful psychological material needs a different kind of approach. It needs to be explored. Listened to. We need to feel into how it impacts us, physically and emotionally. You cannot just let go of it, but once it is really met and resolved, *it* will finally let go of you.

Digesting the Story

That is what all painful psychological material most essentially wants. It wants to be welcomed and listened to. And the beautiful part is, as soon as it finally gets that care and attention, it begins to soften and open up. This is an immutable law of experience. Whatever you really attend to will begin to change. Whatever you care for transforms. Guaranteed. And conversely, whatever you push away will keep on returning. It's like pushing against a coiled spring: the more you push against it, the more it pushes back. But all the force with which it pushes is only the force you are giving it through your own pushing! Your pushing *reinforces* its power. The moment you stop pushing, *BOING!* It moves, releases its energy, and is still.

We are deeply conditioned to push against our uncomfortable experience. We try to forget our pain and "Move on." We tell each other that "Time heals all things." But if you don't resolve difficult experiences and emotions, you really don't move on. They get somatized, stored as unconscious tension patterns that keep you both feeling defended and anxious. This is equally true of very old conditioning and of difficult events that arise anew for us.

Zen and the Art of Crashing a Motorbike

In my mid-twenties, I had a motorcycle accident on a dirt road in France. The bike slid out from under me on some wet leaves and hit a tree sideways. The handlebars dug into the ground, pinning my lower leg below them as the rest of me went over, snapping my tibia, which allowed my knee to bend at such an improbable angle that I actually kicked myself in the face as I went over. I sat up and pushed the bike off me, to find my left leg folded at an impossible angle beside me.

In the next few adrenalized moments, I sat up and rearranged my floppy limb, accompanied by strange crunching noises and searing pain. Then I began to call for help. I was found sometime later by some local hunters and eventually made it to a hospital, where I assumed my obviously broken leg would be set in plaster and I would then be sent home. I was due to travel to India four days later for a month-long retreat, and as I waited to be examined, I imagined what combination of meditation cushions would allow me to sit in meditation with a leg in plaster. I hoped I wouldn't need to lean against a wall (mostly because I was quite judgmental of others who did).

X-rays showed I had snapped and displaced the two knobs where the tibia meets the knee joint. I needed metal plates and screws to hold it all together, sixteen days in hospital, and a further two months of rest, then rehab. India was clearly off the table.

And the point of the story? During those days in hospital, while I could feel my surgery scar and the bones knitting together, I could also sense how the pain of the accident was still in my nervous system. Held by memory as traces of fear and tension. Each time I replayed the accident in my mind, I would flinch and contract physically as I recalled the intense pain and resulting shock. So I replayed it over and over as a visualization, remembering every detail right down to the sounds of the bike hitting the tree, the smells of damp leaves and petrol. With each replay I would sense deeply into my body and breath, noting and softening the tensions that arose. I did this until I could recall the entire process without any flinching, staying relaxed in my body, calm in my mind, at ease through the entire memory sequence. And once I had done that, I knew clearly that I had really resolved the accident and there was no physical or emotional residue.

This process can be helpful with either recent or long-past emotional pain residue. I have given this practice to people many times. In an accident like that, where a lot happens quickly and there is pain, shock, and disorientation, it is almost impossible to process it in real time. So it's impossible to simply "move on." Instead, you need to "move *in*." To go into the story consciously, and into the way that the memory is stored somatically. This is a good example of how we work psychosomatically—accessing and resolving psychological material by meeting and treating it in bodily experience.

You may notice I have not used the word *trauma* in regard to the above. This is because I don't want to cheapen it. I hear people speaking of trauma or of "being traumatized" in increasingly light or glib ways. My laptop's built-in dictionary defines it as:

noun (plural **traumas** or **traumata** | ˈtraʊmətə |)

> **1.** a deeply distressing or disturbing experience: *a personal trauma like the death of a child* • emotional shock following a stressful event or a physical injury, which may lead to long-term neurosis: *the event is relived with all the accompanying trauma.*

There are degrees of trauma, and you have to see for yourself what your resources are when practicing in the way described above. Where memories are severely painful and shocking—truly traumatic—then it may be too much to handle alone and would be better resolved through an accompanied process with a therapist, counselor, or contemplative teacher who can figuratively hold your hand through it. This accompaniment is an invaluable, and sometimes absolutely necessary, support. The most hardwired, painful conditioning is usually relational, and the resolving of it therefore works best in a relational process.

The Way of Resolution

The habitually reinforced material of our sense of self opens up in several different ways. Some reinforcements go in a bang. Some painful patterns are seen so well, so clearly, that resolution is just . . . done.

Maybe you have had a moment like that, where you can just tell that something is resolved in the moment of understanding it, and you know this by its continued absence from that moment onward. Like a visitor who spent decades knocking at the door of your awareness, you finally answered, let it in, listened to it, and learned from it—and now it has gone forever.

The first time this happened for me was around a certain kind of harsh self-talk. I would sneer at myself in a condemning manner whenever I made a mistake. But I didn't see how destructive, how hateful that was. I felt *deserving* of my own opprobrium. Then one day, I just saw it clearly. It was back in India in the early 1990s. I had spent the day meditating in the forest and walked back to the small cabin I was renting on a hillside. Fumbling with the awkward padlock, I dropped my key and as I bent down to retrieve it, I suddenly noticed the hateful nature of my mind-state:

"Why are you so clumsy? If you were really mindful, you wouldn't have messed that up. What's the point of spending the day meditating if you can't even be properly present to open your door? Do you think the Buddha would have dropped his key?"

It was so shocking to really see this in action: to feel the poison of it in my nervous system, to feel, most of all, how I believed my own inner tyrant. And not only in this moment, but to instantly see how it connected back through a lifetime of speaking to myself in this way. And to the origins of that, to having internalized it from having been spoken to that way as a child.

I slumped inside my door and wept. I wept for the harshness of the voice, and for the one who had been spoken to in this way. I wept for a life lived under that spell, and for the fact that suddenly, it didn't need to be that way anymore. That harsh one was blown away in the moment of clear seeing. And I can honestly say that from that moment onward, I have never spoken to myself as harshly or unkindly again. There were more layers to understanding problematic self-talk (this isn't the last we've heard about it, just wait for the next section on self-judgment), but from that moment onward, my inner dialogue was friendlier.

That particular sneering condemnation was gone.

CULTURAL, FAMILIAL, PERSONAL: LAYERS OF CONDITIONING

Other types of conditioning are more pernicious and may need repeated meetings to resolve. They open up by degrees, and we find ourselves circling back around to the same material again and again. There are cultural, familial, and personal layers to our psychological patterning, and we'll explore each of them in turn. We'll use sex as an example, first because we have already explored it a little in the chapter on the instinctual drives and second because sex is such a compelling theme, yet receives so little attention in most meditative traditions.

For each layer—cultural, familial, personal—I'll offer a little context, then give you some journaling reflections to consider. Use them as a contemplation on your conditioning—taking in the questions and writing out whatever comes. Don't censor yourself. Let the thoughts, feelings, and associations flow. And as you write, give particular attention, as we've been emphasizing all through the book, to the feelings that arise and to how they are experienced in your body.

The tendency to want to look away from the difficult areas of our psychology is one reason why it is really helpful to reflect in written form. The writing keeps you on track, keeps you connected to the material even when your attention wants to wander away.

Just see what associations come to mind when you read the word: *Sex*. Say the word. *Sex*. Hear the word. *Feel* the word. What do you notice? What images arise? What associations reveal themselves, and are they related, for example, to pleasure and intimacy or to fear or shame?

First then, the cultural layer: I've had an interesting opportunity to see how values and attitudes to sex are culturally shaped, through teaching a course called *Work Sex Money Dharma*, which I've led in various cities including London, Paris, San Francisco, Copenhagen, and Jerusalem. The course gives people a way to bring their contemplative practice right into the midst of the most charged areas of their everyday lives. Attitudes toward sex vary hugely. I grew up in the UK, where cultural attitudes are still influenced by Victorian prudery, British reserve, and that depressing theatrical title, *No Sex Please, We're British*. In contrast, I have lived for twenty-five years in France where there is a kind of cultural pride around a lack of sexual hang-ups. And in Copenhagen I found a fairly direct, easy relationship to sex, where people were more willing to speak about their sex lives than in other places.

Religious conditioning is also part of that cultural layer. Whether you grew up directly or only obliquely influenced by religion, how might religious views have shaped your feelings and beliefs about sex?

Journaling Reflections

What cultural/religious conditioning have you inherited and might still be carrying, having to do with sexuality, sexual orientation, and sexual identity?

What religious values might you have internalized, either by aligning with them or pushing back against them?

What reactions are provoked, or what associations do you have, with words like *monogamy—masturbation—queer—promiscuity—orgasm—transsexual*? Does any fear, shame, confusion, or embarrassment arise? If so, can you feel into where that comes from?

HOW FAMILY CONDITIONS US

The next layer is familial conditioning. In my own family, sex was very taboo as a subject—barely mentioned or accompanied by extreme discomfort. I inherited very conservative ideas of gender roles and sexual orientation, and it took much reflection and exploration as an adult to recognize how strong this family influence was. Conversely, my family environment was also very loving, stable, and trustworthy, which was also part of that conditioning. My parents gave me really good modeling* for commitment, stability, and care in a long-term relationship.

Exploring sexual conditioning can be both powerful and painful. Sexual violence and abuse, whether in childhood or adulthood,

---

* Hi, Mum and Dad, I'm sure you're going to read this at some point!

affects a tragically large number of people. We looked earlier at the need for sensitivity in exploring trauma, and it is with this caution in mind that I offer the next reflections. You can use these questions as contemplations, as material for journaling, or to explore areas that may need a greater degree of support and holding through some therapeutic accompaniment:

Journaling Reflections

What were the attitudes to sex in your family? Did they conduce ease or discomfort? What healthy or unhealthy patterning was there and how might you still be carrying that now?

When you bring to mind the sexual conditioning of your early family life, what do you notice in your immediate experience? What happens in your body? What associations, images, and memories stand out? How might these associations still be coloring your sexual attitudes and relationships now?

HOW WE REINFORCE OUR OWN CONDITIONING

And what of our personal conditioning then, on top of all the rest? As we saw in the previous chapter, we first have our biological / instinctual conditioning, generated over millions of years of evolving *Homo sapiens*. Then our psychology is formatted in layers—through culture, family background, and finally the personal beliefs and activities with which we express, reinforce, and continue to mold our conditioning.

So how does your own sexual conditioning get acted out? Reinforced? Explored? Digested? Most people's conditioning plays out unconsciously, and they may spend their whole lives unaware of how they are being shaped by their past impressions, and then continuing that shaping on their own in the present, thereby shaping their future patterns. By contrast, any truly transformative practice is one in which we actively engage with our conditioning—first to understand it, to make it conscious, and second to then metabolize it, so that it is no longer the driving force of our beliefs and actions.

If you want to see your personal conditioning in the arena of sex, then look at your sex life! What is your style, as a lover and a partner? Most of us recognize the ways in which our sexual relationships follow certain repeating patterns. We use sex as an attempt to get all kinds of emotional needs met. Also, we easily find ourselves replicating early relationships through our choice of sexual and romantic partners. The old adage that boys marry their mothers and girls their fathers is just a little simplistic, but in many cases quite accurate.

Journaling Reflections

What quality are you most looking for in sex (e.g., intimacy, safety, being dominated, asserting control, being taken care of, merging, etc.)?

What qualities do you expect or hope for in a romantic partner? To what extent do you make them responsible for your emotional well-being?

In which ways do you feel misunderstood, dismissed, or unloved by your partner if you have one? What qualities in a romantic partner most provoke your reactivity when you perceive them as absent?

LAYERS OF CONDITIONING

You can explore any area of psychological conditioning through these different layers—most especially the strongly charged themes like sex or your relationship with money—your sense of right and wrong, or your beliefs about what happens after death. When you know there is something you are strongly patterned by, some area where you get caught in reactivity, take some time to tease out the ways it has become reinforced.

First, feel into the cultural attitudes around the theme. *What have you inherited from your cultural worldview?* Let yourself be present in your direct bodily experience as you reflect. Notice what associations or memories might arise. Be particularly interested in any emotional nuance—frustration, impatience, anger, righteousness—that might be provoked as you explore.

Then consider the family conditioning. *How did your parent(s) hold this? What seems to be their own conditioning in this area? What have you internalized from their influence?* Sibling relationships can be a big factor here, as can grandparents or other influential early caregivers, including schoolteachers and neighbors.

And then, *what has crystallized as your own personal beliefs and behaviors?* Sense into your psychological history and the way you hold the issue now. How does the particular area of your psychology play out in the different areas of your life—such as with your family or at work? And as you explore, what do you feel? Do any uneasy emotions arise, like restlessness, impatience, rigidity, or anger? Do you find yourself wanting to avoid the subject, giving your attention to something more pleasant or reassuring?

JUST THE WAY I AM

These various layers of conditioning run the whole depth and range of our psychology. They make up not only our sense of ourselves, but our modus operandi, the ways in which we think and feel and react to various situations, from the small and everyday to the major themes and relationships of our lives. With such potent impact, these psychological patterns are not usually resolved in a single flash of insight (as we might like!), but rather with repeated exploration. This requires a willingness to keep sensing into the psychological tension patterns that we experience not just as ideas and beliefs about ourselves and others, but which we can also feel somatically. We quite literally "hold" our beliefs, and we can feel that holding as we go again and again into our felt experience, our bodily relationship to our psychology.

Sometimes there's a certain reluctance to enter "yet again" into some part of our inner terrain, especially if, like old, well-trodden ground we have been over it many times before.

I was guiding a student recently in her practice when it became clear that some unresolved resentment toward her father was reinforcing a certain self-view. When I asked if the situation reminded her of her relationship with her dad, she became frustrated: "I don't want to go back into that story. I feel like I have told it so many times." And it is true, of course, that we have all told our story until we are sick of it, to ourselves or others or both.

We become afraid then, that if we acknowledge there is still something unresolved there, it will somehow invalidate all the work we have already done—but actually the opposite is true. The fact of having already explored certain material is how you become familiar with it, enabling you to go back in with clearer eyes and a more open heart. Because if you still get reactive around something, then there is still more to understand. If you still get upset with your parents, there is more work to do around your relationship to them. If you still resent your past, it still has a hold on you. In which case, it needs a little more exploration. A little more gentleness. Once again, it's all about care and attention.

If some reinforced material can vanish in a moment of clear seeing, and other material gets slowly diminished and resolved over time, is there any conditioning that just endures? Is there anything that is unresolvable?

Maybe. Our basic personality is such primary patterning that its fundamental shape or structure is basically with us for this life. Last year I spent a very fun weekend in Paris with a group of friends with whom I was very close at school. Having shared our adolescent years of confusion and lust, intoxication, and a search for meaning, we met up thirty years later and spent a wonderful couple of days reminiscing, laughing, and walking around the Père Lachaise cemetery reflecting on our mortality. One friend I hadn't seen since I was eighteen years old, preparing to go to India, and he was much amused by the story of how I had, in his words, "gotten into meditation and become some kind of guru." Reflecting on the thirty-year gap in our friendship and the decades of meditation and many other associated transformative practices, he put his arm around my shoulder and said, "You know, you haven't changed a bit!"

And that is kind of true. That eighteen-year-old sense of self is a far-off, distant memory now, and though I feel a great deal of affection for him, I am also immensely grateful to have grown far beyond that anxious, confused, and impulsive fellow. My basic personality traits, however, have not really transformed. It's more that they have freed up. There is more space around them, and around the sense of self in general. So I no longer hold myself so tightly, don't take myself so personally, and therefore the stuff of being human isn't so sticky.

Extrovert or introvert, cautious or headstrong, stubborn or easily swayed—you too can probably recognize yourself across the decades, even if you have done much important and transformative inner work. This reveals an important point about transformation: *There is nothing to get or get rid of, nothing to reach for, nothing to resist.* We are invited to meet, welcome, and enter into our material. If we can do that with real presence and curiosity, then transformation will happen by itself. You can get busy trying to "let go" of whatever you don't like about yourself, but those things won't let go of you. But stay close, stay curious, and as you understand your psychology better, those patterns will open up and lose their power over you, dropping away until they are memories, mere ghosts of that person you used to believe yourself to be.

A line often vaguely (though possibly apocryphally) ascribed to Buddha says, "From complete and unexcelled Awakening, I gained absolutely nothing. But let me tell you what I lost: Anger, anxiety, insecurity, and fear." This points to an important distinction in how we approach our inner material. As our habitual dramas and defenses and deficiencies drop away, we meet ourselves more freely. Rather than being constricted by all our self-views and habitual self-reinforcement, we discover our humanness anew in each moment and interaction. Instead of maintaining a belief in myself as "Martin," constantly trying to reinforce that self-image, my sense of self relates more to just this location where awareness and experience are constantly meeting, embracing, dissolving. Instead of trying to shape my personality into some idealized version of myself, I allow myself to be shaped by life in each moment. And this shape turns out to be infinitely malleable. It is awareness-shaped, which is both full and formless.

Invisible, yet right here.

Empty, yet containing all that appears and disappears.

GROWING OLDER, GROWING WISER?

Unchecked, our conditioning keeps getting reinforced.

And the more years pass, the stronger the reinforcement gets, because whatever you feed, that's what grows. If you don't start to explore and undo these habitual reinforcements, they get a greater and greater hold over you. Look at older people who have done no liberating practices. Physical tensions, views, beliefs—all get more reinforced, more rigid. So we keep doing that throughout our whole life, or at some point we wake up to the fact that we are prisoners of our own psychology and do something about it. Habit takes you toward ever greater reinforcement of familiar views of self and world. Authentic awareness practices take you in the exact opposite direction.

For most people, aging makes their world smaller and tighter, their views narrower, their existence more limited. Yet the opposite is possible. We can open up as we get older, growing genuinely wiser as we discover a relationship with life that is natural and unreinforced, open and alive to each moment. This is the difference between conscious and unconscious aging.

YOUR MONEY AND YOUR LIFE

Our relationship to the world of things is yet another self-reinforcement mechanism. We could call it "acquisitive identification," the attempt to reinforce self-identity through getting, having, achieving, becoming. The belief that I am somebody because I have this or that thing, or role, or capacity. My house, my possessions, my wealth, or status somehow prove it and give me a sense of self-importance, however tenuous. And I want you to believe it too, please, and reflect back to me how impressed you are: "Do you know who I think I am?"

Contemporary culture is so consumption-oriented, it is hard to see any other signposts around us that point to a deeper way of meeting life. This was profoundly confusing for me as a teenager. I looked hopelessly through one shiny university prospectus after another, unable to find any pointers toward the great mysterious depths of being human. Adolescence is a time for many of deep existential questioning. Suspended uncomfortably between the two worlds of childhood and adulthood, teenagers are thrust into their age of majority not knowing who they are, only that there seems to be someone they are supposed to be. This can be both exhilarating and uncomfortable. It can be channeled in powerful ways, but the confusion and disorientation easily lead to classic teenage experimenting in ways that are often more self-destructive than self-examining.

Fortunately, there are many more signposts for the current generation. Nothing is further than an internet search away. If you grow up plagued by anxiety, or questioning your sexual identity or orientation, or consumed by existential doubt (as I was), it is wonderfully, mercifully easy to find out that you are not alone and that others share your questions and concerns. The mainstreaming of mindfulness practice has opened the doors of contemplative practice to millions of people who would otherwise never have encountered it. Meditation classes are increasingly being offered in schools and colleges, and there are various wisdom books aimed especially at the bewildering world of adolescence.

For the most part though, our cultural signposts (education, advertising, politics, economics) all indicate materialism as both the primary vehicle for pursuing a "successful life" and the principal measure of it. You only have to look through those ghastly celebrity magazines, full of the dramas, divorces, and drug addictions of what my teacher used to call "the rich and shameless," to see that wealth and status have no real link to ease, peace, and well-being. It is painful, trying so hard to shore up your psychology through the acquisition of mere "stuff." While we have managed staggering levels of material development, our commodification of happiness has led to epidemic levels of obesity, depression, anxiety, addiction—and most pressingly, to an ecological crisis, which is somehow simultaneously desperately urgent and yet mostly willfully ignored. We are so busy trying to consume satisfaction, to reassure ourselves that we are OK, and to prove to ourselves that we exist, we collectively jeopardize the existence of life on earth.

Reflection

What is your own link between your sense of self and material wealth? What relationship is there between who I am and what I have?

EMBODIED PSYCHOLOGY

We have seen myriad ways that our sense of self gets reinforced. Despite the shaping from our history, however, all the influencing factors of your life are right here. Some people speak of the past as distant. "That's all behind me now," they might say. Except it isn't. Your psychological past is not actually behind you. It is in you; it directs your thoughts and feelings; it plays out in the defenses and desires and distractions that make up your habitual responses; it is stored in your bodily experience.

And that is where we meet it: In the immediacy of direct experience. The details of the past are indeed long gone, and no amount of mental replaying and "if only" scenarios can change what happened to you. The emotional residue of the past, however, stays alive in us, ignored yet calling for our attention, until it is actually met, explored, and resolved.

We speak about our psychology as if it were something mental, something that plays out on some mysterious plane, distinct from physical life. The Cartesian split describes a body and a mind, suggesting a separation that is fundamentally untrue: Show me a body separate from a mind, and I'll point out to you that it is a corpse. If you are alive, then your body and mind are inseparable, and the most direct and powerful psychological work you can do is that which plays out in embodied awareness, where your body and mind yield themselves up to an all-inclusive, unifying awareness.

Self-Judgment

Dharamsala, India, 1990: I've just finished a ten-day introductory course in Buddhist meditation. It has blown my mind. My purpose, direction, and values have all completely shifted, and the compass of my heart now points in a totally new direction—toward the True North of Awakening. I'm incredibly inspired by the knowledge that I can explore consciousness, bring awareness to my habits and beliefs, do the work of growing up psychologically and waking up spiritually.

Full of ideas about the nature of self, reality, and awakening, I walk down from the monastery through the fragrant, sunlit cedar forest to the small hut I am renting. The door is made from flattened two-gallon oilcans, nailed to a wooden frame and locked with a length of chain and a padlock.

I feel for the key in my pocket. I'm thinking about meditation and how long it might take me to get enlightened. I take out the key and feel its smoothness and coolness and weight in my hand. I congratulate myself on being so present to the feel of the key as I insert it into the padlock. In the semidarkness I fumble, missing the keyhole and dropping the key. And that's when it starts:

"You're so clumsy. You can't even unlock a door. You can't get a key into a lock without dropping it. And you call yourself mindful?

Do you think Buddha would have dropped the key? What is the matter with you?"

In addition to the words, there is a tone of disgust, derision, contempt. This inner voice is incredibly familiar, so much so that I normally never doubt its authority. Yet today, I hear this voice in a totally new way. In a moment of clarity, I suddenly see that this is not "the truth" about me—the way I am. It is just a voice. A narrative. A habit. An inner structure. A conditioned response. All my life I have given that voice an unquestioned authority over me. No wonder I have been miserable—I've been belittled, derided, judged, and condemned by a tyrant of my own making.

I stand in front of the door, frozen by this sudden insight. Suddenly this inner judge looks weak, small, a little pathetic. I have the peculiar experience of one part of my mind (awareness) clearly recognizing another (the inner critic). This shifts the inner authority over my experience. Wisdom now has the upper hand. I gaze at that neurotic part of myself that constantly worries, doubts, and criticizes, and in doing so, I somehow know that it will never again have the upper hand.

I feel profoundly relieved. Liberated. Exhilarated. I retrieve my key and open my door. I sink down on my sleeping mat and cry for many minutes—partly tears of joy for the ease and inner kindness I have suddenly discovered, partly tears of sadness for the inner tyranny that has held sway for so much of my life. There is relief and joy and forgiveness and sadness. The heart is singing its song of freedom.

Don't *Should* on Yourself

Most of us are incredibly, unhelpfully, and unnecessarily hard on ourselves. We compare ourselves to some idealized version of how we think we *should* be and then complain, criticize, and castigate ourselves for not being that. In the story above, I was using the Buddha as that inner ideal: *Do you think Buddha would have dropped the key?* Do you see how unhelpful that is? And how unfair?

Let's look closely at the psychological structure of self-judgment—what it is and how it operates, how it got formed, and how we can get out from underneath it.

Self-judgment goes by many names: Buddha called it *Mara* (literally, "the killer"), and in the hymn "The Lord of Dance" Jesus tells us, "It's hard to dance with the Devil on your back," pointing to the same structure. In psychological language it is often called the *inner critic*, or as Freud named it, the superego (*Uber-ich* in German, literally the "Over-I").

Way back at the start of this chapter, we explored how the ideas, images, and patterning of our psychology get formed through *self-image*. Then we saw how we reinforce it through various layers of conditioning, or *self-identity*. *Self-judgment* goes way beyond the first two psychological mechanisms we have looked at. Self-image deals with how I see, describe, and think of myself. Self-identity deals with how those ideas and images get reinforced and acted out. Self-judgment though looks past the sense of who and how I am, leaning into the tortuous territory of who and how I *should be*. Entering the inner battlefield of *should*, as we'll see, takes us into a fight we cannot win. Self-judgment is where we tie ourselves in knots of self-doubt, where the self not only describes itself to itself, but then evaluates, measures, and criticizes itself for being that way.

Ouch.

THE SELF TALKING TO THE SELF ABOUT THE SELF

On meditation retreats, I often invite people to consider those around them with whom they have been sitting for the week or so of the retreat. During the days, people build up a deep sense of empathy, community, solidarity, and support as they sit alongside each other, sharing the aching knees and wandering mind-states, as well as moments of deep peace or revelation. I ask them to notice how they speak to themselves about their practice during the retreat days, encouraging or criticizing themselves, measuring or shaming themselves. I ask them to imagine turning to the person next to them in the meditation hall and addressing them in a similar way:

"You don't look very mindful."

"You're hopeless at meditation."

"What's the matter with you? You're so lazy/agitated/stupid. You'll never be able to do this."

"It's a waste of time, you meditating. Why did you even bother coming here?"

Of course, they would *never* speak to their neighbor in that way. It is painful to even *consider* speaking to someone so harshly, aggressively, dismissively. Yet that's exactly how they've been speaking to themselves—the same accusatory stance—the same harsh tone—the same intolerable pressure and intolerant attitude.

Is that familiar to you? There are endless individual variations, but they all boil down to the same thing: We treat ourselves badly. Each of us is, quite literally, our own worst enemy.

Yet it doesn't have to be this way. Real psychological maturation is when we outgrow our inner critic. I've worked with this for decades with many hundreds of students, exploring how it is possible to live with a foundation of deep trust and confidence in oneself—to rely on your direct experience instead of inner criticism, to be grounded in what *is* instead of your ideas about what should or could be. We can be free from the inner critic, but first we need to understand how it formed, who it is, and why we give it so much authority.

GETTING TO KNOW THE CRITIC

As a child, you were deeply impressionable.

You absorbed behaviors and emotions from your parents, siblings, caregivers. How they related to you taught you how to relate to you, and how you relate to yourself as an adult is the direct product of that. Your memories now of early authority figures are key in unpacking your psychological relationship to judgment. As you reflect on the following questions, take care to remember not only the story of what happened, but also to recognize and sense *how you felt*, particularly if you can feel the sense of smallness, confusion, lack of confidence, and so on, that typically characterizes places where external situations became internalized.

How did the early authority figures in your life relate to you?

Was one or another parent (or both) particularly harsh or demanding? Critical? Impatient? Dismissive? Too busy to listen to you?

Was there a dominant elder sibling who made you feel impossibly smaller and less than them? Was an early schoolteacher overly severe, critical, or pressurizing?

Were you criticized for your appearance, or your memory, or your school results?

Were you made to feel wrong, or bad, or stupid, either by inference or being called those things, maybe repeatedly?

Conversely, you may have rather been encouraged and pushed: "Go on, that's easy for you. You can do it." This sounds much better, but encouragement can also get internally felt as pressure and interpreted as inadequacy. If a child is told that something is easy and they should be able to do it, but the task doesn't *feel* easy to them, then they will tend to internalize the blame—*the parent says it's easy, so it should be. I don't feel it is easy, so I must be wrong. I'm not good enough.*

Some parenting is cruel, negligent, or spiteful—the parents taking out their own unresolved pain on their children. Much parenting is well intentioned but inevitably imperfect, as with overly pressurized encouragement. You see this for example when a child hurts themselves, and the parents, wishing to alleviate both the child's pain (and unconsciously, their own anxiety or distress about it), will minimize the child's experience: "Don't cry. It's nothing. You're a big girl/boy now, you shouldn't cry over that. Be brave."

Children thus learn both that their pain or distress is unacceptable and also that they should displace it and disconnect themselves: "Have some candy. Look at what Mummy is doing (let me distract you)."

However well-attuned or mis-attuned the parenting you received was, there are times when you (along with every child ever) felt misunderstood, excluded, ignored, hurt, confused, unloved. One of my teachers used to speak about this absolute inevitability, adding, "...unless you were parented by perfectly awakened beings." Truly, though, I would say this is true *even if* you had these hypothetical buddha-parents. It is just part of forming an adult personality. We learn to measure ourselves by how we were measured—to evaluate ourselves in a way that is limiting, but totally normal. Freud called it the "Over-I" because it becomes the organizing structure for how we experience and describe ourselves.

A Brief History of Everything . . . about You

So much for the generalities—what about the particulars? *Your particulars.*

You recognize the influence of self-judgment and free yourself from its tyranny, by exploring your own history. I want you to reflect on your history, so as to uncover the ways you were blamed or shamed, encouraged or belittled. You probably have particular childhood memories of painful moments when you felt wronged or punished. When painful memories stay with us, it is because the emotional residue of them is yet to be resolved, as we've seen previously, and these memories are a helpful place to start as you unpack your self-judgment history:

Reflection

Which memories stand out from childhood? How did you feel in those moments? As you recall them, notice what happens physically. Do you feel any heat or contraction? How does it affect you now?

We'll deepen this inquiry by looking at the whole structure of the inner critic from several angles, getting familiar with the particular way you yourself get caught in self-judgment:

WHO, HOW, WHERE, WHEN?

1. Who?

For some of us, the inner critic is an internalized parent—as if mum or dad accompanies you internally, commenting on and evaluating you in the ways you experienced as a child. For others, the inner judge is a composite figure, made up out of various authority figures in our lives. It may also be a nonhuman figure, some kind of demon or monster. For others it seems to be oneself, presenting as simply the truth about who and how you are. And inevitably, that's a harsh truth—a description of you that shows up your faults and imperfections.

Reflection

Whose criticism formed your own self-judgment? Who is it that appears as the voice of evaluation, telling you how you should be different or better, blaming and shaming you for not being that? What gender is the voice? Is it recognizably a he or she, or a nonhuman "it"?

2. How?

Self-judgment takes different forms for different people. Most commonly it is an inner voice, which probably has a tone you recognize from childhood. It may be angry-shouting, or whining-nagging, or undermining-belittling. For some people it is more of an inner atmosphere than a voice. There is just a feeling of wrongness or shame or fear or threat. This may be especially true for those who lived in this kind of home environment as a child, where judgment was implied and acted out rather than spoken.

There are typical psychological responses when under attack from the inner critic—habits of childhood experience. Sense for yourself: You might feel small or helpless, fearful or vulnerable, defensive or defiant, furious or impotent. The more easily you can find out how judgment affects you, the easier it is to recognize it when it happens.

Reflection

How does self-judgment show up for you? Is it predominantly as a voice or an atmosphere? If the former, then what tone does that voice have, and what is its effect on you? If an atmosphere, then what is the feel of that and its effect? In either case, what happens to you when self-judgment is activated? How do you see yourself?

---

3. Where?

The demon of self-judgment has a location in your experience. You can find out yourself where you experience its presence. Here are a few classic locations for where the inner critic shows up:

In your head. Tuning in to judgmental thoughts, many people experience them, along with all their other thoughts, as happening in their head. While there is a correlation between the electrical impulses of brain activity and the production of different types of thoughts, it is too much to say that thought "happens" in the head. Thoughts are mysterious, and after thirty years of tracking my own thinking, I can categorically state that I have absolutely no idea where thoughts happen, other than "here." If judgment feels like it's happening in your head, notice what kinds of tension happen, both there and elsewhere in your body.

On your shoulder. As in cartoons, many people experience the voice of judgment like a whisper in the ear, an insidious form of compulsion to be a certain way, to do certain things, to conform to certain ideals. Bullied by your "shoulder angel/devil," you can be made miserable by trying to satisfy its endless demands. Self-judgment is experienced in this way especially in its whining form—an almost continuous litany of *could-should-ought to.*

Standing over you. When I started exploring this form myself, I realized that I heard my inner judgment as if a large authority loomed over me, like Gerald Scarfe's Schoolmaster in Pink Floyd's *The Wall.* It was a voice that screeched at me and waved its cane, threatening pain and punishment, showing contempt for my perceived deficiencies. It was deeply shocking and saddening to see how cruel and sadistic he could be and to recognize how long and how fearfully I had lived under its influence.

Reflection

Where does your inner critic live? Does he/she/they/it appear internally or externally? How big is it in relationship to you? The more authority we attribute to the critic, the bigger it is in proportion to us. As we reassert our own inner trust, the proportion changes, until it appears smaller and less powerful than our own sense of ourselves. That is when it really loses its power over you.

4. When?

The inner judge can feel for some like an almost constant presence. Look carefully, though, and you will find how it comes and goes—how it gets triggered, and crucially, the moments when despite your feeling about its constancy, it is actually absent. Everyone has some moments of ease and basic confidence, and getting to know these moments consciously is extremely helpful as a reference for what it is like to be free of self-doubt—you get to know your self-judgment *by knowing its absence.* This is an embodied practice. You let yourself feel the ease and fluidity in your body when you are not second-guessing yourself. The kinds of activities that allow this ease can also become good ways to re-orient yourself when caught up with the inner critic.

I have a friend who is quite painfully nervous and ill at ease socially. He is also a skilled musician, and when he plays, you can feel all his doubt and discomfort vanish. He trusts his fingers, trusts his ear and the inspiration of the moment. Music is a realm where he finds an ease and confidence that often eludes him elsewhere, and I have been encouraging him to use that feeling consciously as a resource.

For me, swimming gave me this feeling when I was little. I felt free in the water in a way that I somehow never did on the earth. I was a chubby, asthmatic child and often felt uncomfortable in my skin, but swimming allowed me to feel graceful, powerful, capable. Find something that gives you this kind of free feeling and use it as a resource.

Equally important is to get to know when judgment is present. It may be certain types of relationships that bring it out, when, for example, you are in the company of someone you feel intimidated by. It might be when you feel exposed and vulnerable, or it could happen more when you're alone. It might arise more strongly with someone you wish to impress, etc. Finding out when you are most liable to a "superego" attack helps first in learning to recognize it as just doubt, rather than the truth, and second in then being able to engage some helpful strategy, several of which we'll explore as we go on together.

Are you getting a sense of your own patterns of judgment? Having explored your history a little, I'd like you to look at how you hold your own habits of judgment and how to put them down.

Reflection

Where do you have a taste of this freedom in your own life? What situation, relationship, role, or activity allows you to be completely unencumbered by self-judgment? It might be walking alone in nature, it could be a relationship with a very close friend, or it might be some aspect of your work or a hobby or sport.

What situations provoke your sense of doubt and deficiency? Which relationships make you feel lesser, and how are you evaluating yourself in contrast to the other person? When do you pressure yourself to be different or "better" and feel that you are somehow deficient, wrong, unwelcome, or unlovable?

THE JUDGMENT VORTEX

Self-judgment operates in three distinct loops: self to self, self to other, and other to self. We have focused until now on the first, where you tell yourself stories about how you are and should or shouldn't be. In contrast, self-to-other judgment goes outward, evaluating others. Some people feel they are more judgmental of others than of themselves, but if you look carefully you'll see it's basically the same process. However we judge her, him, or them, it is always in relation or contrast to oneself.

I was recently exploring this with a student who told me she doesn't really judge herself, but can be very critical of others. I asked her to notice what her own sense of self felt like in the moment of judging others. In our next meeting she recounted how she felt herself harden, feeling both superior and defensive at the same time. These qualities may be subtle, but if you start really noticing, that's what is happening every time you inwardly condemn or dismiss someone else.

Sometimes you may feel wiser, wittier, and generally better than others.

This is more uncomfortable to acknowledge. It is easier to own up to judging yourself as deficient than as arrogant and inflated. *I feel unworthy and undeserving, I feel small or incapable or unlovable* is much easier to say, and to hear, than *I feel entitled, I feel bigger and better and brighter than everybody else.*

THE TYRANNY OF COMPARISON: INFLATION AND DEFLATION

Grandiosity is more compelling than self-flagellation, but it is still a limited and intimately painful view of oneself. If you tell yourself you are bigger or better than others, *notice what that feels like.* It literally feels inflated, puffed up. It takes a lot of energy to maintain, and it feels inherently insecure—because actually, it is not true. Whether you see yourself as better, worse, or the same as another, whether you build yourself up or to put yourself down, you still make yourself into an object to be endlessly and usually brutally judged. Decide you are better than another, and you live with a distasteful sense of inflation and arrogance. Judge yourself as worse and you feel deficient and worthless. Make yourself "the same as," and you flatten out the inevitable and important differences that make us uniquely fascinating and valuable.

Reflection

How might you meet yourself if you were neither better nor worse nor the same as anyone else? What kind of dignity and care might you afford yourself and others if your judgment was suspended? How do you feel right now, if you don't judge your experience as right or wrong?

The third form occurs when you project judgment outward, imagining what others are thinking of you. This is based on two delusions: (1) that the person really is thinking whatever you have made up, and (2) that whatever you imagine they are thinking is something really true about you.

For some people, this realm of myriad imagined views is the primary way self-judgment operates. You may find yourself scanning the room at work or in social situations, telling yourself all kinds of stories, making up a whole narrative about who and how you are, told through the imagined views of those around you.

Sometimes of course, the judgment of another is not simply imagined. Someone may insult you to your face, telling you their own judgmental perceptions. If you believe your own self-judgment, you end up colluding with the other person's view—add the other person's view to your own and it seems like corroborating evidence against you. Actually though, like a rope you mistake for a poisonous snake, the judgment of another is only as painful as you make it with your own collusion.

Reflection

How do you think you are viewed by your friends, colleagues, lovers, family? How do you think you're neighbors think of you? What about people in positions of authority—your boss for example? Are these ideas based on clear truths or built up by your own projected judgment?

A MEMORY

Thai Monastery, Bodh Gaya, India. Mid-1990s: I'm on a month-long silent meditation retreat with my primary teacher, Christopher Titmuss. Every few days we have meetings with the teacher in small groups. Eight of us crowd into his small hut. We have known each other for several years, sitting on many retreats together, and have become close friends.

During the meeting, I try to explain something about my practice and understanding to Christopher. He looks at me witheringly and replies: "Never mind your insight. What about your lack of it?"

I am devastated. I feel hurt and misunderstood—ridiculed in front of my friends and rejected by someone whose approval and respect I desperately want. When the meeting ends, I go out into the monastery gardens to practice walking meditation, feeling hot and agitated, angry and defensive, full of ideas about how I have been badly treated.

I keep replaying the story of what happens, and it gets a little more distorted and grotesque each time. I am inventing a relationship where my teacher hates me and my dearest friends are all laughing at me. I am telling myself painful stories about how they all view me—and I am living in the nightmare produced by those views.

I lie down under my shawl and sob. I feel wretched and alone. Whatever poise and spaciousness I thought I had found in my practice has evaporated with the heat and intensity of the situation. I have become a total prisoner of my own judgment of myself.

A few hours later I am still feeling miserable. One of my friends from the meeting comes to see how I am. She tells me that she saw my shawl heaving on the lawn and went to tell Christopher that "since our meeting, Martin is outside crying on the grass." He responded with a gentle smile: "That's a good, healthy flow of the emotional life."

After hearing this, and as the day went on, I began to see how much pain and drama I had created for myself. I started to separate out his one line of commentary from all the ways I had used it as a stick to beat myself. I felt how harsh I had been. I saw how my own cruelty to myself outweighed anything he or anyone else had ever done to me. As I replayed the situation, my harshness softened. I began to treat myself kindly, seeing how hurt and confused I had been. I stopped replaying the conversation, staying instead with a kind awareness of my current emotional state. I started to feel a strong sense of inner gentleness—respect for my experience and gratitude for the whole situation.

At sunset, instead of taking my tea up to drink on the roof, I waited outside Christopher's *kuti*, and when he came along, I bowed deeply and thanked him. He whom I had taken to be the source of my pain, was actually the catalyst for my healing.

We don't have to collude with whatever we hear about ourselves from others. We know this even from children's playground verses:

> Sticks and stones may break my bones,
> but words will never hurt me

But to establish some real space from that collusion is easier said than done. Some lines from the beginning of *The Dhammapada* (in the translation by F. Max Müller) point to how you can remain genuinely nonjudgmental toward yourself, regardless of what is said and done around you and to you, holding others' views lightly—lovingly even:

> "He abused me, he beat me, he defeated me, he robbed me," in those who harbour such thoughts hatred will never cease.
>
> "He abused me, he beat me, he defeated me, he robbed me," in those who do not harbour such thoughts hatred will cease.
>
> For hatred does not cease by hatred at any time: hatred ceases by love, this is an old rule.

And I'll add, in the same spirit:

> "She doesn't like me. They don't approve of me. He's more beautiful/smart/wise/spiritual than me. They are wrong and stupid and I am right and better." Those who harbour such thoughts reinforce envy, jealousy, self-criticism, or righteousness, all of which are forms of self-hatred.
>
> "She doesn't like me. They don't approve of me. He's more beautiful/smart/wise/spiritual than me. They are wrong and stupid and I am right and better." For those who see clearly through such thoughts, there is no basis for envy, jealousy, self-criticism, or righteousness, and all hatred dissolves.

GETTING OUT OF YOUR OWN WAY

Colluding with others' views is painful. Seeing them as simply views is liberating. So what can you do to find and stabilize that kind of clarity and ease?

There are a few particularly helpful ways to get the devil off your back, whether it appears in the loop of self to self-judgment or bound up with your judgments about others or theirs of you.

In the Buddhist texts, Buddha speaks about the night of his awakening and his encounters with Mara, the Buddhist personification of greed, hatred, and delusion. After six years of pursuing various yogic and meditative practices, he sits down with the resolve to understand the essence of human life and liberation and is first confronted with lust and sexual desire (described as Mara sending his daughters to dance naked in front of Siddhartha). Then there is the physical discomfort of sitting in meditation posture for a long time—portrayed as Mara firing arrows at him as he sits (upon arriving they turn into flowers, signifying the meditative ease and equanimity where unpleasant sensations cause no reactivity and a deep sense of peace can be maintained even in the presence of discomfort). Then, Mara employs his most powerful tactic—he approaches Siddhartha as the voice of doubt: "Who do you think you are, sitting here? Why do you think you could understand anything profound? What makes you special? You'll never understand anything!"

Ouch! Maybe Siddhartha's inner dialogue as he sat there wasn't very different from yours or mine when we have doubted ourselves. It's here that Siddhartha gets knocked off balance, showing the pernicious power of self-judgment. He opens his eyes in order to see if there is more to his experience than just his own doubting thoughts. He touches the earth to feel the support of life. He recognizes his right to be here, just as he is. He regains his composure.

The earth-touching gesture is immortalized in many Buddha statues, and it points us to a potent way of working with self-judgment:

He opens his eyes: Look around you. Ground your attention in the sensory immediacy of this moment as a way to get out from the inner vortex of your own doubtful and critical thoughts. Come to your senses.

He touches the earth: Right now, in this moment as in all others, life is supporting you. The earth is holding you up. Air is keeping your cells oxygenated. Your consciousness is switched on. Just you being here is the total proof of life's support for your existence. Feeling the truth of this support, in your own body, in your breath, in your belly, is an incredibly powerful foundation for reestablishing a certain basic trust in life. It allows you to relax into unmeasured experience and establishes your right to be here, to be who and how you are. Right now. Like this.

You may not reach out and actually touch the earth with your hand, but you can feel your feet on the ground. You can take your attention *down*, from your racing thoughts into your legs and feet. You can sense the support of the earth and know it as yours. You can establish, in any moment, your basic OK-ness.

"I see you, Mara." It's an intrinsic part of the human condition— noticing what's happening and producing a view about it. The *tendency* for self-measurement is an integral part of being self-aware. Mara shows up all through Buddha's life, but the structure gets more and more obvious and no longer causes him any trouble. Whenever Mara makes an appearance, Buddha clearly recognizes him as the voice of self-judgment. He meets him with a warm, easy smile, saying: "I see you, Mara." When judgmental views are seen like this, they lose all their power, and Mara collapses. When Buddha recognizes Mara in the texts, his game is up: Seen thus, Mara slumps his shoulders and slinks away.

This is the most powerful, straightforward, and simple way to see through self-judgment. "I see you, Mara." I see that these thoughts are unhelpful, unnecessary, untrue. And I'll just leave them alone. I give Mara a warm smile, and he slinks away. Judgment dissolves. Effortlessly.

You can practice this in everyday meditation, in that moment where you notice you've been caught in thought—that's actually a great moment. It's a cause for celebration. You were totally lost in thought, but life's immediacy is way more powerful that your abstract thought-world. No matter how far down the rabbit hole you've gone, life's immediacy wakes you up out of your reverie. You've been brought back to presence. (You couldn't do it yourself because you were too busy thinking!) Then, what happens in that moment? What do you do about the fact that you are suddenly awake again, here again? The opportunity is to be gracious and grateful—to recognize and delight in your good fortune: I'm here ... woken up out of my reverie! If that moment of recognition is corrupted by Mara's influence, then how easily we make it into a stick with which to beat ourselves:

"Oh, I was caught up again."

"I can't even be mindful for one minute."

"Oh, I was thinking about that thing again."

Whether that inner voice is harsh and cruel and cutting, or relentless and nagging, or blustering and angry, or whether it's not even a voice, just an atmosphere of disapproval or disgust—recognize your own judgment style right there, from however you felt negated, criticized, shamed, encouraged, pressurized, blamed, and evaluated when you were young. "I see you, Mara."

Just say no: Sometimes it is not possible to be that gracious with your own mind, particularly if you are just starting to work with this material. We have learned to accord Mara so much authority, that he/she/it seems big and you seem small. It seems right and you feel wrong. When this is the case, you need to take back authority, to trust your seat. This is another version of touching the earth, of reclaiming your right to your experience.

A friend of mine once dated a woman who, when she disagreed, would hold up her hand in a STOP gesture, look witheringly at her interlocutor (usually my unfortunate friend), and say, "Talk to the hand, 'cos the head ain't listenin.'" That's not such a nice way to speak to a lover or a friend, but it can be a *great* way to speak to Mara. You refuse to engage. You just say no. You take back the authority over your experience. You hold up your hand and say *Stop*. Like Gandalf on the bridge in *Lord of the Rings*, facing down the enormous fire demon, planting his staff between them and roaring, "You shall not pass!"

Humor: When we start to really get to know Mara, we see that we have been caught in a kind of tragicomic drama in which we play both hero and villain. Much of the problem is that we take ourselves so seriously. The inner critic seems real and right *only because we believe it* to be so. Humor explodes this mythology by seeing that the emperor has no clothes.

When I first recognized this severe schoolmaster figure looming over me and pronouncing judgment on my thoughts, speech, and actions, it was shocking to see how much power I gave it. Yet I also started to feel how much effort that took, how much work it was to maintain this strict and unforgiving taskmaster. I imagined that underneath the long black robes, Mara was wearing red-and-white polka-dot underwear. Suddenly he was a comic figure, a kind of grotesque clown. Why would I take him so seriously? I imagined him on the beach in a deck chair in his spotty shorts, taking a well-earned holiday from his main job of harassing me.

What about the character of your inner critic makes you take it so seriously? What might burst its bubble, collapse its authority? How might you see it as a figure of fun?

As with all ways of getting space from the inner critic, the essential thing is to redress the power balance, disempowering the judgment and empowering your basic sense of OK-ness. I've encouraged students to blow raspberries at Mara or to metaphorically put their fingers in their ears and blow it a big, insouciant kiss.

Mockery also works well for some people. You might experiment with sending the judge out of the room: "That's great that you have such interesting ideas about how I should be. Let me show you into the garden now so you can criticize the trees."

"Thanks so much for your insights about how poor my meditation practice is. Please do your own absolutely perfect meditation over there, while I stay and do my own low-grade practice over here."

Exaggeration: Amplifying Mara's rhetoric can help you to see how absurd and distorted it is, especially when you start to have a clear sense of your inner critic. You sit back and let it rant, turning up the volume on its complaints and criticisms in order to see through them. What started as doubt about your meditation practice because you weren't very concentrated becomes the absurd statement that you are the very worst meditator in the world. The concern about whether you appeared rude or aloof or preoccupied or boring at that social event last night becomes a surreal tirade about how you are a total sociopath and nobody in the world will ever want to speak to you. Importantly here, you are *not* reinforcing the self-judgment. You are showing yourself how out of proportion it is, as a way to release it, to ignore it, to let it moan away in the corner while you pay it no attention.

THE DEMONS OF *ALWAYS* AND *NEVER*

Nothing is constant. Mind-states and inner narratives come and go like clouds in the sky. If your inner rhetoric is speaking in absolutes, it's a sure sign that Mara is around:

I always make a mess of things.

I never manage to say what I mean.

I'm always afraid of appearing stupid.

I never know when to keep quiet.

I'm always distracted.

I never take enough care.

I always go too quickly.

I never remember to be mindful.

When students come to me with stories of *always* and *never*, I ask them to attend carefully to the moments when a particular problem or pattern is absent. The impression of constancy makes patterns seem intractable: *It's always like this* is never true or helpful. Notice your critical thoughts. Look out for beliefs in *always* and *never* and feel the effect of their seeming solidity. Look into your experience in different moments to find those that defy the views of constancy, and use those moments to undo the judgmental views about how you *always* or *never* are.

NO REHEARSAL, NO REPLAY

Here is a practice I often give students to help undo their allegiance to their inner critic. You give attention to how you habitually anticipate or *rehearse* a particular scenario, and then also to how you analyze or *replay* it afterward. And then you practice doing *neither*: no rehearsal, no replay.

No rehearsal doesn't mean you can't write a speech you are going to give or reflect a little on what you want to say at a difficult meeting. Rather, it is stopping yourself from imagining: *How will I be? What will they think of me?* And so on. You don't let your mind go down that road. Or when you notice that despite your best intentions your mind *has* gone there, you stop. Just as in meditation when your attention has become caught up in some abstraction, you unhook. You leave that thought-stream alone. You start to see that the rehearsal is just a way of judging yourself *in advance.* It creates anxiety and a familiar, limited sense of yourself, ahead of time, in a way that then becomes self-reinforcing. So you make a practice out of dropping the rehearsal. Prepare what you need to, without reinforcing your self-judgment.

No replay means you make a practice of refraining from going back over *what I said, what they thought, what I was like.* Replay is never objective. It is distorted by the lens of the mind-state through which you are looking. Each replay adds a layer of distortion until you have no clear view anymore over what happened or how you comported yourself. Replay your experience through an anxious, doubtful, or critical mind-state, and you will literally construct the evidence for your own inner trial and conviction by self-judgment. Once you have spoken or acted, leave it alone. If you are left feeling doubtful about your experience, attend to the doubt itself—*care for the feeling instead of meddling with the story* of what happened.

This practice is simple and powerful. Refrain from rehearsing and replaying and you will remove much of the cause of anxiety and doubt, you will increasingly trust your experience, and you will find your wisdom and clarity in the moment of speaking and acting.

A Grain of Truth

We stay entranced by self-judgment because we feel it somehow encapsulates the inherent truth about us. We are so accustomed to Mara's "moral guidance," we fear that without its authority, we will go astray:

If I no longer evaluate myself, who will keep me on track in my life?

If I don't scold myself, I won't be a better person.

If I don't keep myself in check, all my worst instincts will be uncontrolled.

This is why it is so important to establish an inner confidence and trust in your experience. When you become your own authority, you no longer need to listen to Mara's fear-mongering.

And yet, sometimes Mara has a point! It is true that we can speak and act in ways that are unhelpful or unkind—it may be equally true that it would be good for you to be a little more disciplined in your meditation practice, that you would do well to be cleaner or tidier at home, or that it is worth making more of an effort to not be late for work or friends.

So, when you see these or other truths about yourself, how do you learn from your experience without falling into Mara's trap of berating and belittling yourself? The crucial difference is what you are evaluating: wisdom reflects on your *behavior*; Mara judges your *identity*.

A student spoke to me about this recently, concerned that without Mara's censure she would somehow lose her moral compass. She mentioned an example where she had spoken angrily to her partner, expressing her frustration and irritation in the guise of arguing about some domestic matter. I asked her to tell me about the situation, exploring her reactivity without forming an ego-judgment. She made an important distinction between remorse and guilt: the former helps you reflect on your unskillful actions and is very useful—the latter judges your self-worth and is always use*less*:

Guilt: "I spoke harshly. How could I be so horrible to someone I love? I should have apologized. I should never have behaved like that. I'm always so reactive and vengeful. I hate the way I am. How can I have been so hurtful to one I love?"

Wise remorse: "I spoke harshly. I feel sad about upsetting someone I love. I would like to apologize, and to behave differently next time. I can see how that was reactive and vengeful. I can feel how it hurt both me and one I love."

Please, for the sake of your own heart and well-being, learn this distinction. It is crucially important. It makes all the difference between learning from your mistakes and punishing yourself for them.

You can also practice with this in how you speak to others, especially in your family, and *most* especially with your children. As we've seen, the way children are spoken to becomes the way they will speak to themselves.

You can let them know that their behavior may not be OK, without giving them the impression that they *themselves* are not OK:

Judging parent	Skillful parent
You're so messy. You need to tidy up your room.	Your room is really messy. I want you to tidy it.
You're so easily upset. Calm down. Don't be a baby.	I can see you're really upset right now.
That's so easy. Come on, anybody could do that.	It looks like you're unsure of whether you can do it? What might help?

I have worked with hundreds of students in person and online in discovering, engaging, and dissolving their dependence on self-judgment. There is a huge scope to this work. It underpins all other real transformational practices, because unless you have woken up to and at least softened the impact of self-judgment, it will undermine all the other breakthroughs that you make, sowing seeds of doubt, dispute, and disappointment in yourself. I have a six-week online course that goes into this material in great depth and detail, at MartinAylward.com/i-see-you-mara/.

BEYOND THE PSYCHOLOGICAL SELF

We've explored three key elements of the psychological self: self-images, self-identity, and self-judgment. In the midst of all this psychological complexity however, right now you are right here, *just like this*. Sense your experience for a moment, as you sit here digesting the material we have been exploring. What is your sense of self like right now? We tend to inhabit our experience as if we're in control of body and mind. Beneath this facsimile of ownership and control however ("my body, my mind, my life!"), you might genuinely ask yourself, *Who am I?*

This physical body has its own intelligence and rhythms. It also has its inherited instincts, to which we're held hostage by our evolutionary imperatives for survival, sex, and social recognition. Those in turn are overlaid with our psychological mechanisms. This sense of *who-I-am* with which you sit, is conditioned, contrived, and constrained by all these layers.

At the same time, that means that the confluence of all that conditioning is *right here*. Here in this body, in this situation, in this moment. Right in the middle of this biological, instinctual, psychological material is where all possibility exists. Here is where you meet yourself. Here is where you engage with and explore your experience. Here is where understanding develops. Here is where the liberation happens.

So stay here. Please. Don't abandon yourself.

Hang out in the moment-to-moment experience of bodily life.

Notice how the self-images arise so you can see through them. Notice the identities you reach for, and leave them alone. Watch the habitual judgments that Mara lays on you, and disengage from them. Stay present in the totality of your experience, so that it can become more open, more accessible, more free.

5

An Awakening Body

We are extraordinary beings. We are so used to our human functioning we take it for granted: this human body-mind here, in front
of a laptop screen, tapping keys and writing thoughts, and your
human body-mind reading and taking in these words. Illness or
injury may wake us up to the fragility of our bodies—if you've ever
broken your leg and been on crutches, you'll remember how suddenly walking is recognized for the miracle it is. But unless an issue
becomes chronic, we easily drift back into complacency when the
condition heals. (When it *heals*! That is also pretty extraordinary).

My teacher Christopher Titmuss, during his six years as a monk
in Thailand, was given a daily practice of slowly raising and lowering his right hand, repeatedly, and contemplating the process (for
three hours, every afternoon!). Contemplating doesn't mean thinking about it, imagining sinews and muscles, synapses and "orders
from the brain." To contemplate the fact that the body moves at will
(moves at all!) is to wonder deeply at the miracle we are.

You can take a few moments to contemplate:

Reflection

Rest your hand on your lap. Then raise it and lower it slowly a few
times. If you leave aside your ideas and explanations, can you tell how

it happens? Feel the movement from the inside. When we suspend our knowledge about this body, we can enter into its mystery. Maybe we don't know this living, breathing body at all well. A deep relationship with body is not at all what we may think it is.

Six Ways In

Buddhist meditation uses six particular ways to enter into and contemplate bodily life. Like an explorer venturing into unknown terrain, we enter the mysterious universe of own inner life, with awareness as our compass and these six maps of bodily experience to guide us through our felt terrain. These have been dealt with in great depth and detail by other writers from Buddha on down through twenty-five centuries of commentary and analysis. Here are some brief notes on each.

1. This Breathing Body

I had chronic asthma as a child with a few acute attacks involving nighttime blue-light-siren, oxygen-mask ambulance journeys to hospital. When I began to meditate seriously at age nineteen, I was used to carrying an inhaler constantly and needing it frequently. Breathing had been a source of fear, restriction, and panic since I was seven, and this lent an extra layer of challenge to "mindfulness of breathing." During my first three-month retreat in 1990, I breathed into layers of defensiveness in my chest. As I felt the historical constriction in my chest, I found emotional nuances of feeling suffocated in my family. I found how tightness in my chest, as well as compromising my breathing, was an unconscious attempt to control my experience—particularly my emotions.

Breathing is amazing. After thirty years of meditation it is both deeply familiar to me yet still, of course, always new. Each breath has never been breathed before. Each breath is configured differently. Enter deeply into breathing and you are confronted with the nature of all things—subtle, changing, ephemeral, ungraspable, freely unfolding.

You are not "the one who breathes." If you were in charge, you wouldn't last five minutes! You'd forget. You'd fall asleep. You have plenty of other things to do. Yet the body breathes. You might take that for granted, but contemplate it awhile and you may find yourself in deep awe and wonder at the genuine miracle of a living body. Attending closely and daringly to breathing is the deep foundation of really inhabiting bodily life.

Reflection

Take a few moments to sense into your breathing.

Feel the movement and energy of the in-breath—that expansiveness that oxygenates the cells.

Sense deeply into the out-breath—that natural quality of a certain relaxing, a letting go, a coming to rest.

Notice also that momentary still point at the end of the out-breath—sometimes just a flickering moment before the next in-breath—sometimes (increasingly, as our familiarity with it grows and as our breathing rhythm relaxes and slows naturally) offering a taste of a certain vast, wide-open, empty stillness.

Keep noticing. Use the expansiveness of each in-breath to increase your sense of presence. Use the relaxation of each out-breath to rest more fully into your experience.

Notice if you are holding any unconscious tension patterns in your body, and if so, see if they can soften, relaxing into the next out-breath.

You never really get used to breathing. You can't. Each breath is over in a moment and then there is a new one to get used to. Sit steadily and sincerely again and again with your breathing, and your life will change. You'll be more sensitive to your inner experience. You'll be quicker to recognize when you are getting tense, reactive, or defensive. You'll be less fooled by your own mind. You'll be more at home in your body.

2. Sitting, Walking, Standing, Lying

Somebody once asked Buddha, "Do I have to be mindful *all the time*?" His reply was something to the effect of: Just when you're sitting. Or standing. Or walking. Or lying down. Or moving between any of those.

These four are the postures for formal meditation practice. You can meditate in any posture, but they are not the same and they cultivate different qualities:

Sitting: The posture of impeccability. If you think of meditation, this is what comes to mind. A beatific yogi, legs crossed elegantly and effortlessly, calm and bliss writ gentle upon their face. The reality, of course, is somewhat different. To sit in meditation is to sit in the fire—to lean into your experience, to face your discomfort, to cultivate presence in the face of all that pulls at your attention.

Standing: The posture of no escape. I struggled a lot with standing meditation when I began practicing. I learned to sit without too much discomfort, sometimes distracting myself with some pleasant reverie. I learned to at least *look mindful* in walking meditation, even if I was spaced out. But standing posture gave me the powerfully uncomfortable sense of being very directly confronted with myself and having *no escape*. One postural thing that helped was softening my knees, rocking my pelvis gently until I really felt my spine to be well aligned and upright, shifting my weight from my heels, where it went by habit, to the balls of my feet, which brought more energy, lightness, and brightness. The other thing was using the sense of no escape so that I grew to love the poise of standing. When I am on retreat I use standing to lengthen the time of uninterrupted formal practice. When my legs become too stiff or uncomfortable, I shift to standing for a while, then back to sitting.

Walking: The posture of reflection. On all the month-long retreats I attended in India through the 1990s, I'd see Christopher walking up and down in the monastery gardens at dusk every evening before giving his daily Dharma reflections. He presented brilliantly and compellingly, synthesizing and advancing ideas, drawing on anecdotes and examples, challenging us to fulfill the promise of an awakened life, here and now. He spoke without recourse to any notes, and when I asked him how he prepared those talks, he said it was by walking up and down. Walking meditation, he said, is conducive to reflection and insight.

I've found that to be exactly so in my own practice. If you want to really enter into some theme of contemplation, exploring it viscerally *and* reflectively, then the gentle rhythmic movement of the body walking helps to discharge any restlessness, leaving the mind clear for reflection. Eyes are open (of course!) in walking practice, and that also contributes to reflection. Whether it is a formal practice of walking up and down slowly on a short path or the more informal evening stroll with the dog, walking seems to create conditions for clear thinking, inspiration, and making cognitive connections. Inspired by Christopher's example, and then because I found it really works for me, this is also how I spend the minutes prior to giving teachings.

Walking is also a really helpful posture in public places. During the morning rush hour, train and subway stations seem to exude an oppressive vibe of impatience, stress, fatigue, and grumpiness. Yet there is a lovely, long straight platform to walk up and down on, as if offered on purpose to the meditator. The ends of platforms usually have room even at the busiest times, and I find it both soothing and empowering to walk up and down in the minutes before the train arrives. Soothing, because as mentioned above, walking discharges restlessness and agitation. Empowering, because in the very midst of that agitated psycho-sphere, people's unconscious dissatisfaction bouncing around the ether, one is present and poised, receptive and gentle, honoring this moment of experience and this human life.

Lying down: The posture of surrender. The clue is in the name— the posture of surrender. Reclining in lying-down meditation, one literally has *nothing* to do. No effort to make. No muscular integrity to maintain. You can let your limbs be heavy and soft. Let the bed, or floor, or grass, hold your resting body. Let go, completely.

Lying-down meditation can be especially useful if you *have to* lie down to meditate, perhaps because of spinal injury or chronic fatigue issues. To prevent falling asleep, if you are lying on your back you can raise one hand—your elbow on the ground with fingers pointing upward. If your hand drops, you'll notice and it will show you that you were going dull or falling asleep.

Unless you are doing *all* your meditation practice reclining (missing out on the impeccability and clarity of the sitting posture), personally I don't think there's anything wrong with sleeping! For some people, cultivating the gentleness and restfulness and ease of lying is particularly helpful. On retreat, I encourage people to rest as much as they wish or need to—in any moment, in fact, except for the formal sitting and walking sessions and during teachings.

One of my first teachers spent some time training in a Zen monastery in Japan where very particular emphasis was given to "every-moment-Zen." One morning his teacher asked him—"Last night, did you fall asleep on the in-breath or the out-breath?"

Conscious lying-down practice can simultaneously cultivate deep relaxation *and* great brightness and wakefulness. One puts aside all concern with whether or not sleep will come and just allows all bodily control to relax. To support letting go of even very subtle tensions, some like to scan through the body in different ways—top to bottom or up one side and down the other—sensing into each area, feeling the sensations there, and inviting them to be at ease.

Taking time to lie down consciously is deeply soothing for the nervous system. I travel between time zones a lot to teach retreats and spend much of my life jet-lagged. I try to lie down for twenty minutes or so after lunch every day if the situation permits. It feels like one of the best things I can do for my nervous system and overall health, whether sleep comes or not.

Sometimes when you lie down, even though the intention is to relax, you can feel the momentum of the day buzzing in you. You feel energetically over-caffeinated. Tired, but wired. The mind is busy, the body is agitated—rest won't come. The mistake is to try to *make yourself* calm down. Instead, see if you can just attune to the agitation. Sense into the electric feeling in your body. Try to track the general restlessness of your mind, rather than fussing with the various bits of mental content. This way, feeling the agitation without feeding it, you give your nervous system the chance to self-regulate, to slow down naturally. When you stop feeding a fire, the flames will die down by themselves. If you do this several times, you will start to be skillful with meeting agitation and letting it subside.

3. Moving and Acting

This third way into embodied awareness is basically *mindfulness in action*. Any action. *Every* action. Inhabiting your lived experience. *Being where you are.*

At first, being present seems like hard work. It is easier to be spaced out or caught up in some inner drama, and it takes huge effort to haul your attention back to here and now. But as we explored earlier (in the chapter "This Human Body"), it is being caught up that is actually stressful. Being present is mostly characterized by relaxation and clarity. Presence can become easeful, natural, and near constant.

The more present you are, the more awake you become to your various habits—your compulsions, contractions and confusions, your fixations and self-importance. This is about more than simply *me being aware*. You naturally begin to question what you do. Try out some of the following questions as you go about your day:

Reflection

What do I give energy and attention to?

What am I hoping for from various actions?

What is the impact of my actions on myself, others, and the environment?

What might I believe about how I behave and speak that might not actually be true?

How much do I rush unnecessarily?

How attentive am I to the people around me?

The Art of Slowing Down

Most people, most of the time, move more quickly than they need to. I'm not talking about running for the bus—I mean operating with an internal imperative, an over-revved engine, an agitated nervous system and an overactive mind which makes you drum your fingers while you wait for your coffee order, fidget with your phone when there is nothing you need from it, walk as if rushing because, well, just because it's your habit. Moving quickly, while stressful, gives us a sense of purpose, as if pace and posture are saying: "Look how busy and important I am; I have no time to hang around." "I have so much going on," we boast to each other, as if we would prefer it to be otherwise. We tell each other: "I really need some *space*," but as soon as you have some free time, do you just sit there, surrendering to the void? No, you fill it up with *doing something!*

Slowing down is an art and a practice. When we first moved to Moulin de Chaves, the meditation center in southwest France where I live and teach, the four floors of the main building had no rooms. No doors. No floorboards. No ceilings. We got busy renovating, planning retreats and managing the administrative and legal affairs, and during the first weeks there I would often find myself running up the four flights of stairs. My thoughts would already be at the top, fixated on where I was going and what I needed to do when I got there. And with the body playing catch-up, I'd be rushing up and leaping down the stairs all day.

Seeing this, I made a practice of slowing down. That doesn't mean I never ran up the stairs, but I practiced *not letting my mind leave my body*—not getting ahead of myself. That one mindfulness exercise changed how I went through the day. The body relaxed a little, which was easeful, but more significantly, the mind slowed down. The inner *relationship* to moving and acting and doing changed. I felt more spacious, less rushed. I entered into that mysterious and counterintuitive truth, that when you slow down, you have *more time.* Which doesn't mean your clock moves any differently, but time is actually subjective. Rushing reinforces the sense of time pressure. You feel squeezed, busy, harassed by time. Slowing down conduces to ease, gentleness, relaxation.

Until you really give attention to this, you probably don't realize how much you rush. We even try to make tea quickly, though you cannot make the kettle boil faster. One of my teachers used to tell me, "There's no such thing as waiting for something else."

There may be good reason to move quickly. There is never good reason to rush.

Reflection

Notice how you go up stairs. Or make tea. Or brush your teeth. Or get dressed. Or wash the dishes. Or do your grocery shopping. Feel for the inner imperative that makes you feel busy. That compresses your sense of self into a forward-pushing agent called *me.* Focused on what I'm doing and where I am going. What happens if you soften and slow, just a little bit? Feel how that changes your experience. Your sense of yourself. Your capacity for ease in the moment.

The Most Important Thing

With embodied presence in your movement and activities, you also see what you give most energy to. What habits you feed. You see what you make most important and whether your intentions—*what you want to be your priority*—and your actions—*what you actually make a priority*—are aligned.

Shunryu Suzuki Roshi, author of *Zen Mind, Beginner's Mind,* says that the most important thing is to find out what is the most important thing! Most people only have vague ideas about what is most important to them. If you don't know, how you can you support what is most important?

I have a student who loves meditation. He comes on retreat. He reads Dharma books. He's deeply inspired by the stories of the great yogis, hermits, and mystics. He tells others about the myriad wonderful benefits of meditation practice. The only thing is ... he doesn't meditate very much! He would *say* it's the most important thing. He will tell you that *you* should meditate. But he doesn't walk his talk very well. There is a big, incongruent gap between his intention and his action. This is all too common of course. It's behind the failure of all our good intentions and New Year's resolutions.

The first step is to find out the most important thing. Of course, it changes with context. The most important aspect of my inner life might be the commitment to meditate each morning. The most important aspect of my relationship may be listening deeply to my partner. The most important part of my work may be bringing honesty and integrity to what I say and do and how I make a living. The most important thing to remember when I visit my family might be to be patient with a relative I know annoys me, or it might be to take care of myself with someone who easily upsets me. The most important thing today might be to get a certain amount of work done to fulfill my commitments, or it may be to take rest and recover from some previous busyness.

So ... What is the most important thing in the different situations, relationships, and wishes of *your life?* And then ... *what do you do to support that?* How aligned are your intentions and actions? Good intentions are easy—the road to hell, you'll remember, is paved with them! Aligned action takes steady, committed, sincere work.

I had the immense good fortune to discover my "most important thing" at age nineteen. Within fifteen minutes or so of hearing my first Dharma teachings, I knew utterly clearly and unambiguously that I would spend the rest of my life with meditation at the heart of things. Suddenly, so much that had been confusing was clear. All the existential bewilderment I'd been experiencing had a focal point. I could free my mind! Maybe it was because I was young and had few other distractions. Maybe it was the force with which those first teachings hit me. Maybe there was enough clarity in that moment to see that if I had the good fortune to find the most important thing, then I better have the good grace to follow through on it. It would be disrespectful to life not to do so—as if I'd been given a precious gift and just forgotten it, leaving it unopened.

The second step is to look at the gap between intention and action. Once you've found *the most important thing* (the M.I.T. in a particular situation or for the whole of your life), it would be a great tragedy for that to be lost amid the various little dramas and details of everyday life that can easily take up so much time and energy. Find the M.I.T., and it's quite easy to relinquish the small stuff. You can let something go graciously when you know you're surrendering it for the depth, beauty, and meaning of the M.I.T.

Embodiment and Mystery

Finally for presence in action, embodied presence brings you increasingly in contact with the fundamental mysteriousness of experience. Earlier I gave the example of just raising and lowering your hand. This is not just about "being mindful" or present in the experience. It can be a profound contemplation about how experience happens at all. Can you really understand the relationship between volition: "I want the hand to move . . . oh, there it goes"—and action? How did the wanting arise? How does the movement happen? *Who or what is the one doing all this?* What keeps body, heart, and mind and all of life animated? It's easy to come up with some answer, but answers are useless. Answers don't satisfy our truly profound questions.

Over time, with this bodyful/mindful practice of inhabiting your movements and activities, you start to slow down, become more sensitive. Your contemplative capacity develops in unimaginable ways: to be curious, to explore your experience directly, to understand in a very immediate, nonconceptual manner—to make connections between *your* experience and *the nature of* experience. Like staying present with your hand. The way one hand rests on another in meditation, as if they are caring for each other, resting on each other. The way hands move and give and receive and act. The feel of my hands moving across the keyboard now. The way hands can be the instruments of our grasping and fighting or of our tending and helping.

Inhabit your body as you move and act. When you're happy and at ease—when you're sad or confused or angry or hurt. Let bodily life speak to you.

4. Bodily Composites

The fourth way to deeply contemplate bodily life is through awareness of the different body parts and functions. The traditional teaching in the Satipatthana Sutta (in Thanissaro Bhikku's transation below) invites us to reflect on the specifics:

> One reflects on this body enveloped by the skin and full of impurity, from the feet up and the top of the head-hairs down, thinking: "In this body there is hair of the head, hair of the body, nails, teeth, skin, flesh, sinews, bones, marrow, kidney, heart, liver, spleen, lungs, intestines, feces, bile, phlegm, pus, blood, sweat, fat, tears, grease, saliva, mucus, earwax, urine.

You recognize body's physical, "meaty" components as a way to loosen the fetishization of youth, beauty, and longevity. Because, let's face it, you're aging, decaying, and you're going to die. (More on this in a moment.)

On the one hand, you have to be careful with this reflection. Culture encourages us to be critical of our own bodies. Media reinforces distorted ideals of physicality, and if combined with unresolved shame and self-loathing, some people hold an painfully unhealthy relationship with their own bodies (often symptomized by things like anorexia, bulimia, self-harm, body-dysmorphic disorder). For those ill at ease with their bodies, it is much better to focus on being gentle, accepting, and gracious toward oneself—a much more helpful practice for those plagued with dislike of or disgust with their own bodies.

On the other hand, seeing meatiness, the flesh-and-piss-and-phlegm-and-shit-iness of the body can help you relax your fixations. For instance: It's normal that the body sweats. Gets spots and rashes. Natural that it ages and wrinkles, aches and stiffens, and decays with age.

Contemplating like this can also awaken you to the miracle of how the body functions *remarkably well*, given how complex it all is:

- The rhythm and movement of breathing, extracting oxygen to feed your cells
- The adjustment to changes in temperature—just a few degrees out either side mean either fever or freezing
- The alchemy of digestion, transforming food into flesh and bone and energy
- The growing (and graying, and falling out) of your hair
- The maintenance work of various organs, filtering impurities, organizing minerals
- The changing, aging, self-repairing, increasingly wrinkling nature of skin
- With so many complicated and interrelated processes going on, the very fact that you are alive at all

I'm sometimes completely awed by the body's natural intelligence: It's doing its own thing. Nails aren't growing on command. I don't decide whether hair will stay or gray or go. If I had to manage all this *myself*, how long would I last? Contemplating like this, the body becomes a source of gratitude and wonder.

5. This Elemental Body

I remember being taught to contemplate the elemental nature of the body in 1990 at Wat Suan Mokh, Ajahn Buddhadasa's jungle monastery in Thailand. The monsoon was due and the air was so humid that nothing ever fully dried. Clothes all smelled of mildew (this wasn't a problem for the bed linen as we slept on thin reed mats on concrete slabs and had wooden blocks for "pillows," considerately carved with a curved dip in each one in which to cradle ones head. Luxury!).

Ajahn Buddhadasa once described Dharma practice as "giving back to nature what we have wrongly appropriated from it," a journey from being the owner of "my" life to an intimacy with all of life. This way of contemplating explores the natural elements—earth, water, air, and fire. You sense into your own experience of the body, to find what it shares with the whole body of life.

As I go through each element, track them in *your own felt experience*, sensing and exploring so that instead of just *reading about* the elements, you can meet them in your own body.

Earth: The earth element is heavy and dense. Feel your butt on the chair, your feet on the ground. Sense the heaviness and density in these sensations, allowing them to *ground* you. Sense deeply into the immediacy of pure physical sensation, and you cannot really find where your body ends and the ground below you begins. You belong to the earth. Your body's nature is earthy. All the solidity and mass of your physical existence has come from earth and will return to earth, through burial or as burned ash. You are not separate from the earth. Not other than earth. You are of the ground beneath you as much as you are of the body that sits upon it.

Water: The water element is fluid. Feel the saliva in your mouth. The wateriness in your eyes. Sense the fluidity that runs through your whole body-field. Everything flows. All experience is liquid, moving and changing, taking on the shape of your consciousness like water filing a vessel, then pouring out again. Sense into the wateriness, the liquidity of all your experience. Let it all flow. Your body is fluid. A newborn baby is more than 90 percent water. You are dependent on water. Dehydration would kill you. You are watery in your being.

Air: The air element is spacious, airy. It is the air constantly entering into and leaving your nostrils and lungs—oxygenating your cells, enlivening your being. Sense your breath deeply, the way the air of "the world" and the air of your breathing are inseparable. Inner and outer merge and dissolve. Feel the space around your bodily sensations. The space between your thoughts. Evoke the open, spacious nature of your mind and all your experience. Feel the air on your skin, the same air that you can sense as breath. Consciousness is like air—invisible yet essential, subtle yet obvious. The air element gives space to all things. Your experience is inherently airy.

Fire: The fire element is heat—the enlivening warmth of your body right now. Sense into that warmth in your belly, the heat at the core of bodily life that keeps you warm, the fire of digestion that transforms food into calorific heat. An alive body is a warm body. Feel that aliveness in you right now as the fire that burns in you as each nerve ending lights up, as each thought bursts into consciousness. The cauldron of your experience is fired by the heat of the world.

Contemplating this way is another way of relaxing the *I, me, and mine* that we otherwise overlay onto our experience—the identification with this body as *who I am.* Instead, let it all be natural. Elemental. Let go of the burden of making it *yours.* Give back to nature that which you have unnecessarily and stressfully mistaken for you.

6. Contemplating Death

Death is most certain.
The time of death is most uncertain.
What should I do?

This traditional Buddhist reflection puts things into perspective. Life is short. How much of yours is already over? Thirty percent?

Fifty percent? Eighty percent? It could already be 99 percent—none of us know if we'll last even the rest of the day.

This sixth traditional practice invites us to contemplate our life in the light of our inevitable death. Traditionally practitioners sit with a decaying corpse, reflecting that this too is their own destiny, as the flesh of the corpse swells and rots, stinks, and gets eaten by maggots.

I've spent many hours sitting at cremation grounds in India and Nepal, watching bodies that were alive just a few hours ago disappear into flames. One time just outside Kathmandu, I remember watching a family arrive with their dead mother. The priests offered chants and blessings—the pyre was sprinkled with incense and sanctified water before being lit. The air was soon barbecue-scented as human flesh sizzled and burned. Boiling blood and burning sinews can cause odd movements, and the dead woman's arm suddenly rose up eerily in a part grotesque, part endearing last wave at her family from amid the flames, twisting at an unlikely angle before sinking back onto her chest, suggesting some final resignation and peace.

I watched for a while (a cremation like this takes a few hours) before walking up into the hills for my daily walk. Hours later I passed again by the riverside ghats, and now, she was all gone. Her relatives had left. Two *doms* (the people who maintain the burning ghats) sieved through the last ashes (looking for gold from her teeth) and then, with a nondescript gesture of finality, swept the very last dust off the cremation platform and into the river. No trace left.

This gone-ness—a woman's life utterly disappeared into an ash smudge by the river—made a profound impression on me. I stopped my walk and stared about me. All I took in seemed simultaneously so vivid and alive, yet also hollow and empty, everything bound to decay and disintegration.

There were several nuances to this. The first was a sense of desolation: Myself and everyone I've ever known and loved and all things that have ever been are bound to this fate. Nothing lasts. Everything is slipping away. Each moment moves us closer to being snuffed out of existence.

I sat down by the flowing river, which seemed to be carrying each moment and all of existence off to its death. I felt my own cells dying, my body disintegrating, my mind failing. Everyone around me appeared as walking skeletons, corpses-in-waiting. I saw stars burning out and the whole unfathomable totality of existence wearing its death mask. I stayed with the rise and fall of my breathing, each exhalation a mortal end, a window into nonbeing in that timeless, still moment at the end of the out-breath where all things cease. Utter gone-ness. This, I understood to my marrow, is where I, we, all of us, are inexorably headed.

In this darkness and nonbeing, I started to see something else. This impenetrable void of nothingness was profoundly still. At peace. A great all-encompassing silence. An end to all agitation and angst. The river still flowed, people moved about nearby, the clouds drifted across the sky, yet nothing made even the slightest disturbance. Everything was rising out of and dying back into the black silent night of consciousness. Peace and stillness enveloped all things. It was clear that the nature of mind is unfathomably empty—infinitely deep—utterly still.

Clocks ticked, yet time no longer passed. And then, within this gone-ness and nothingness, I started to feel a new significance in that I was still breathing. Rising out of the black hole at the end of each out-breath came a new inhalation. Again and again. Life and expansion and oxygen. Creation. A new universe in each moment. Life's very emptiness was also the source of its dynamism and creativity. Each in-breath, every cell re-energized. Each new moment, the world took birth. New sensations. New thoughts. Constantly. And so this tree, that person, the river, as well as being on their way to destruction, were also constantly arriving. Born anew in each moment. While the essence of all things is its gone-ness, bound to death—the *expression* of all things was its *presence*, its aliveness, its utter *here-ness*.

This is the potency of contemplating death. To see how fleeting and fragile this life is, is also to bear witness to how precious and dynamic it is. The only certainty in life is death. And right now, in this space before our inevitable demise, is great possibility. Great aliveness.

How will you make best use of it?

These six ways of contemplating body are profound tools for exploring who you think you are and how you meet your life. The first three usually get more emphasis in meditation teachings, because they are direct embodiment practices—being present in breathing, in different meditation postures, and in moving and acting, respectively. The second three are more reflective in nature—contemplating the body in its parts and functions, elemental nature, and impermanent condition.

MULTIFACETED MINDFULNESS

There are many different modes by which we can give wise, embodied attention to our experience. Instead of reducing mindfulness to simply a "nonjudgmental, present-moment attention," Buddha draws out many different nuances and functions to being present. He variously compares *sati* (the Pali word for mindfulness, presence, embodied attention) to a shepherd resting in the shade of a tree, a military night watchman searching for signs of an attacking army, a charioteer controlling and tempering the passions of her horses, a security guard deciding who can enter and leave an area.

Mindfulness isn't passive, it adapts to circumstance. If all is well—mind at ease and the situation benign—your attention can relax in the cool shade, like the shepherd. Just one eye gently surveying the flock of thoughts, in case one strays to dangerous territory. When you get caught in some emotional drama, your attention may need to be more like the charioteer, pulling on the reins of your wild-horse mind, de-escalating the emotional charge, recognizing and letting go of the drama before it gallops off uncontrollably. At other times your attention might be like the night watchman, watching for attacking thoughts and mind-states. Just as a recovering alcoholic meeting friends in a bar may be attacked by thoughts of drinking, or an unhappily single person surrounded by couples may start to spiral into thoughts of self-pity, in situations where you know your mind is vulnerable, your attention scans your mental landscape for any sign of danger. Then also, your mindfulness may sometimes be like the security guard, keeping watch at the "sense doors" of experience, meeting each thought-visitor as they arrive and using your discernment to see which are worth allowing in and encouraging, and which need escorting from the building.

How Mind Moves

Mind moves in mysterious ways. But as we stay present, we start to understand our patterning. There are three main ways that mind moves and three particular modes we can cultivate by practice.

The first is when mind is *compelled*. Any experience with enough intensity commands your attention. If a firework went off outside your window now, attention would immediately go there. Or if, to use a famous example, I ask you not to think of a pink elephant, then your attention inevitably goes to that concept. If you start to feel cold, attention goes to the experience, followed quickly by the impulse to warm up and the thought to put on a jacket or turn up the heat. Similarly with emotional intensity—if you get upset with something you read, then attention is pulled toward the state, and thought follows to create a narrative: "That's outrageous, how can that person/government/corporation behave like that?" Anytime something intense happens, your attention is pulled there and there ain't nuttin' you can do about it.

The second way mind moves is *by habit*. If nothing particularly intense is happening to compel your attention, it will probably go where it usually goes, like an old dog on a familiar walk. Some of us wander off into the future by habit, to fantasy or worry, building castles in the sky, imagining scenarios we either long for or fear. Others mostly take the winding paths of memory, branching off to either nostalgia or regret, telling ourselves *how it was*, reawakening our otherwise long-dead experience. And others go around and around in the present, narrating, analyzing, and judging whatever is happening right now. All of us know what it is to wander around in these three fields of time, but give close attention and you'll probably find you have a "favorite" direction, a place where habit most often takes you.

The third way mind moves is *by practice*—purposefully directing your attention somewhere useful instead of blindly following compulsion and habit. There are three particularly important "attention settings" for meditative practice: In Pali they're called *vitaka, vichara*, and *viveka*. We'll look at these three Vs as pointing attention, handling attention, and embracing attention, respectively.

THREE TYPES OF ATTENTION

Pointing attention (*vitaka*) is like a finger pointing to a particular object. It's the attention you train in meditation, sending your attention back to breathing when it has wandered off into abstraction. You can't prevent attention moving when it is compelled by a strong sensory impact, but you can radically alter the way your attention moves by habit. Various studies on meditation and neuroplasticity have demonstrated how improved attention diminishes stress, supports well-being, and produces happiness neurochemicals. You can read the work of Rick Hanson, Ritchie Davison, Dave Vago, and others for details. For me personally, it is not the scientific data for how attention can change that impresses me—it is the true raw data—the lived evidence of a clearer, brighter, happier, and more easeful mind.

New meditators often get discouraged by the way their attention gets frequently distracted. People tell me, "I tried meditation once, but it wasn't for me." Well, it's not really for any of us! Mind's habits keep it running around after whatever desire, belief, or opinion pulls at it. The good news is that it doesn't matter that your attention keeps moving. What is really significant is that you keep bringing it back! Every time you intervene with your habit of mind-wandering, several important things happen:

1. You cultivate *clear seeing.* You *recognize* where your attention is. Doing this again and again, you become more familiar with your patterning, more insightful about how mind works.

2. You have a genuine choice moment—to *release* the thought that has snared your attention. You didn't have that choice when your mind was first seduced by whatever grabbed your attention, because you were unaware. But in this moment of presence, you can unhook from it. You can drop the habit, leave the thought alone, be independent from your habitual thoughts.

3. Thus freed from habitual thought streams, you can *return* to presence consciously—to bodily sensation, to the movement of your breathing or your footsteps on the ground. Rather than being pulled along by whatever hijacks your attention, you are now consciously designing—and optimizing—your own experience. You don't choose what happens to you, but you *can* choose how you meet it.

4. You *reestablish* embodied presence. You find your home again, in the open space of awareness, in that poised place right in the midst of your changing experience. From being pulled along by each desire or defense or distraction, you reestablish the opposite—a mind that's *undemanding, undefended, undistracted.* You live, for this moment, in peace with yourself and in presence with life.

I sometimes give these four points to meditators as a practice plan:

Recognize

Release

Return

Reestablish

This is how you train pointing your attention—directing your attention skillfully again and again and again until it becomes second nature to recognize where you are, to release unhelpful or unnecessary mental busyness, to return to life's immediacy, and to reestablish ease and clarity.

HANDLING ATTENTION (VICHARA)

It's extraordinary, the human capacity to explore our inner lives. We can not only experience, but also self-reflect on our experience *at the same time!* And we can consciously develop that capacity, so as to both enter more fully into what is happening to us and to contemplate its nature, becoming the instrument of our own evolution. This extraordinary human capacity needs conscious training, however, because left to our own devices we mostly just fill our heads with mental junk—vaguely recycled memories, vaguely imagined future scenarios, vaguely narrated present moments, and compulsive reactivity to any strong stimuli that come our way.

Handling attention can hold an experience in mind, taking the time to feel its shape, texture, contours. Like that party game where someone is blindfolded and an object is put in the palm of their hand to feel, discover, explore, and name, *vichara* is the quality of attention that explores and *handles* our mental-emotional experience. You get to know your own mind-states intimately. You meet your emotions *from the inside* instead of just through the drama of what is happening. Vichara makes the difference between blaming your partner for upsetting you, for example, and *noticing* you are getting upset, then being able to explore and take care of and understand the emotional state and its origins in you. You feel it, know it, understand it . . . so you don't get into ego-drama with it.

To cultivate deep curiosity is to look into your mind like a mirror that reflects whatever appears in consciousness. Whereas *vitaka*, or pointing attention, is how you can turn and look directly into the mirror instead of everywhere else, *vichara*, or handling attention, is polishing the mirror, studying what is reflected. This is not an intellectual study, though neither does it exclude thought. It is body-centered, "kinesthetic curiosity." Awareness leads, and thought follows. When I meet with students, this is often what we do together. I support them in *inquiring* into their experience. Though people usually start with the ego-drama, of who did or said what, with encouragement they turn from identifying with their emotion to tracking and exploring it.

Reflective thought is an important part of exploring experience, but if thought overtakes awareness, you end up just *thinking about* what happened. When *embodied awareness* leads the inquiry, and thought follows, we discover the art of inquiry.

EMBRACING ATTENTION (VIVEKA)

Mind gravitates to particulars. Like right now, your attention is focused on the words more than on the blank space on the page around them, and on the object of the book more than the empty space around it. Attention locks onto whatever attracts it, and the more intense the impact of the particular object, the more fixated you get, and the more obsessively you think about it. *Viveka* or embracing attention is how you recover a spacious perspective, a wide view. You meet the objects of experience with an open, relaxed, embracing attention—in touch with the detail, but spacious. *Making room* for experience without getting caught up in it.

Most people never really know this quality of attention. They move from one stimulus to another, their attention by turns demanding, defensive, and distracted, reacting habitually and largely unconsciously to whatever is happening, bouncing around at the mercy of habit-flippers in life's pinball game. But if you really train your attention, you can, like the Dude in *The Big Lebowski*, abide. This spacious accommodation of experience is deeply relaxing. It's what is meant by being *in the world, but not of it.* Being intimate with experience, but not caught up in it. It renders experience transparent, so that as Leonard Cohen's song describes, you get "the feel that this ain't exactly real. Or it's real, but it ain't exactly there."

This meditative exercise might give you a feel of this wide-open, embracing attention.

Reflection

Take a moment just to feel yourself sitting here. As you read these words, sense the weight of your body on the chair, and the rhythm and movement of your breathing. Feel your hands and arms. Allow your body to be as relaxed as possible.

Notice how you can stay in touch with these words (both visually on the page and cognitively, understanding what you are reading), while also at the same time sensing your physical sensations. Feel how there is space in your consciousness for both.

Feel your physical experience more fully. Feel the way your consciousness has room for what is being felt. See how you can feel the sensations and simultaneously have space around the sensations—how you can sense your legs, be in your legs, while also resting into the space in which you are feeling. Explore this for a few moments at least.

Now try this visually: First, notice what you are looking at (this book). Now notice the visual space around the book, the space in the room or park or wherever you are. Take your time; see if you can feel as well as see the space around the object.

Now see if you can expand the spaciousness a bit more, sensing the edgelessness of the visual field. Endless space. Wide open.

And finally, see if you can sense the awareness in which your visual field appears—the consciousness which registers seeing—the open, wide-awake, spacious embrace of awareness that can welcome and include all experience.

Embracing attention, by its nature, allows you to relax. To settle into the space around experience. It is the natural resting place of the nonreactive mind. And you can look for it around every experience, in any moment.

THREE EMBODIED INSIGHTS

All the ways we have felt into, explored, and deconstructed the sense of self so far are oriented to one clear goal: liberation. This is manifest in three embodied insights, or three freedoms:

Freedom from compulsion, when you understand how you get caught in desires.

Freedom from contraction, as you can relax unconscious tension patterns.

Freedom from confusion, as you let go of unconscious views and gain a clearer sense of reality.

We've emphasized how this is an *embodied* awakening, there are three core insights that underpin this liberating process—three shifts in how we understand ourselves and reality in significantly different and deeper ways than we were previously accustomed to.

The first shift takes you from body-as-object to body-as-experience. While you relate to the body as a thing, you confer on "these three cubic feet of flesh" an unreal solidity and permanence. In contrast, regarding this body as an experience, in its constantly changing, fluid nature, lets you live as this viscerally felt *body-field*, a field of sensory experience that is constantly both impacting and impacted by all you come into contact with. Like a fish in water, you are wet through and through with embodied presence—intimate with all objects, without holding yourself as a fixed subject. You are deeply at home in your body and all its experiences.

The second shift is from assuming ownership and control of experience to letting it happen by itself. Planets turn, grass grows, breath breathes, and heart beats. Allowing life's naturalness and the body's *natural intelligence* to operate in you (*as you!*) is profoundly relaxing, relieving, and freeing. Rather than assuming responsibility for your bodily life—and by extension for all of *your* life, you instead *let it happen*. You receive rather than direct, you respond rather than react. There is a shift from conceiving of yourself as a discrete being, fixed in time and place, to having neither edge nor center. Search your field of experience, and you'll find no hard edges. Neither your auditory field nor visual field nor feeling-field has any discernible edge. Awareness expands ever more diffusely toward imagined yet unfindable boundaries. Go inward and it is the same. You find ever greater subtlety of sensation and emotion, but no central console, no kernel of self.

With body as a changing field, freely unfolding, edgeless and centerless, your meeting with life inevitably extends way beyond self-preoccupation. *Right here* turns out to have infinite reach, and from now on this is where we are going—beyond the individual and into the collective body—the I in all things and all things in me.

Walt Whitman said, "I am large, I contain multitudes." We are going to meet Whitman's multitudes.

6

This Collective Body

———————◆----------◆----------◆———————

Wisdom tells me I am nothing;
Love tells me I am everything.
Between these two,
My life flows

—SRI NISARGADATTA MAHARAJ

I love these lines above from Sri Nisargadatta Maharaj (1897–
1981). He was a remarkable, nondual Indian teacher from Mumbai,
India, who lived until 1981, and the author of *I AM THAT*, which
my teacher described as "the greatest spiritual textbook of the twenti-
eth century." These few lines from "Mr. Natural" (a rough translation
of his name) remind us we can go beyond a partial, boundaried, limited sense of self, in either direction. You can explore inward, finding
nothing, identifying with nothing, until the sense of self dissolves
completely. This is seeing through the lens of *wisdom*. Or you can
explore outward, including everything in your field of experience,
expanding the sense of self until you identify with *everything*—the
whole cosmos, the embrace of love.

"The whole world arises in this very body." Both the "inner
world" that we call *me*—my body, heart, and mind, my story and
issues and history—and the "outer world" of people, places, and
situations—everything that appears as *not-me*. It's important that

you *can* distinguish between that which is "self" and "not-self," but take your "skin-boundary" to be a fundamentally *true* boundary and you find yourself isolated and alienated from life's totality.

Sometimes that boundary melts exquisitely, revealing a profound intimacy with all that is. It can happen spontaneously, through nature or music or drugs or sex or danger. That intimacy gets consciously cultivated in meditation. Experiences like this show you you're not as separate as you *think* and inevitably raise deep heart questions about our true relationship with each other. How separate are we, really? If I am fundamentally un-separate from all other beings, how do I reconcile the personal concern for *my* wants and needs, with *yours* and *theirs*—all these so-called "others."

This dichotomy plays out socially—we make boundaries not just between self and world but also in the toxic tribalism of *us and them*. Look at the history of war and religion, with its goodies and baddies, chosen ones and heretics. Look at contemporary politics. Look at nationalism and anti-immigrant rhetoric—racism, homophobia, and all forms of prejudice and marginalization. Look at the tragedy of how we demonize each other, blame each other, exclude each other from our hearts.

Tragically, many of us are as yet unable to extend our "us"-boundaries very far. Boundary identification follows a clear developmental progression. It goes from ego-centric—"It's *all* about me"—to family-centric—"I love my family and I'll act to nurture and protect them"—to "group-centric," along more or less tribal lines, whether we identify with a football team, a religious or political affiliation, or a nation-state or ethnicity. Any group that creates insiders who are "my people," inevitably creates outsiders who are not. They are *other.* Different, opposite, and in their otherness they become *irrelevant*, and therefore excluded from my heart. That is how we demonize immigrants, despise our political divisions, caught in the same dynamic that runs from family feuds to geopolitical conflicts.

When I was a teenager, we drew lines of group identity around our taste in music and clothing, marking us as goth, punk, nerd, or the hilariously named modern romantic. Narrow group identity is really an adolescent level of development. A group identity is comforting, but as we are seduced by the promise of belonging to an "us," we don't see the danger of creating a corresponding "them." As you increasingly feel your true body to be the whole universe, all of life present right *here* in your awareness, you can no longer ignore the implications: All beings are in you, and you in them. Your practice has to become one of growing into this collective, inclusive, *infinite* body. We'll explore three aspects of that deep collectivity: solidarity, community, and love.

SOLIDARITY, COMMUNITY, AND LOVE

On meditation retreats, people often have expansive experiences of a deep *inter-being* with all things, touching the truth of Walt Whitman's celebrated line: "I am large, I contain multitudes." These experiences powerfully demonstrate that the "flesh boundary" of *me* and the group boundary of my particular *us* are mere abstractions. We coexist—we *inter-are* (to use Thich Nhat Hanh's evocative term) in deep solidarity with all of life. The trouble with meditation retreats, though, is this: they put a lot of emphasis on meditation! At the end of the retreat, you've heard all these great meditation instructions, but very little instruction for the rest of life. You've now got great guidance for the twenty or thirty or sixty minutes of your daily formal practice, but all you've got for the other twenty-three hours are the two classic all-purpose injunctions: "be mindful" and "be compassionate." Those are great instructions . . . but they need a little fleshing out, and applying them in a messy, relational world with *other human beings* is challenging. We're in a fundamentally nonseparate relationship with at least seven billion other humans, plus all other planetary life, plus those yet to be born, and whatever others inhabit all other realms, galaxies, universes. We've got some serious expanding to do in terms of what and whom we identify with. We need to get our asses from self-centric to family-centric to group-centric to world-centric to cosmo-centric before we run out of time and air and water and space and die, dissolving back in the end into the primordial oneness of all things (life *will* reassert its infinite all-inclusiveness on you eventually, like it or not, even if it is merely in the form of the earth reabsorbing your rotting corpse).

We don't *want* to put others out of our heart. But look at the conflicts in your own life—at work, in your family, and so on. *Any* conflict is dependent on you making the other wrong or bad in some way. Of course, the other is equally convinced of their own rightness, but just as it takes two to tango, conflict only gets a real hold when both parties invest in rightness and wrongness. It is natural to disagree, but when you invest in your own position, you shut down your heart, ignoring Rumi's famous invitation to meet him in that field "out beyond rightness and wrongness."

Maybe your *intention* is already cosmos-centric, universe-spanning. Including all beings everywhere is an explicit orientation in Buddhism, as evident in many verses embodying the practice of loving-kindness, or *metta*:

> May all beings be well.
> May all beings be safe from harm.
> May all beings in all the realms in all the universes
>   know peace and ease and liberation.

But if you're anything other than absolutely limitlessly blown wide open, then you probably have at least some "*us-blindness*," a boundary around those you feel your collective to be. We identify most primarily with what we're exposed to: family, because there's so much shared time and history and experience—then those who are familiar to us through repeated exposure—neighbors, colleagues, those with whom we interact regularly. This is why cities are more liberal-minded than rural areas: familiarity actually breeds acceptance, contrary to the usual expression about how it breeds contempt. If you live in a multi-ethnic neighborhood—if you see same-sex couples holding hands on your street—if you have a transgender colleague—then those things become your normal and enter more easily into the "us" of your collective identity. If you experience only a narrow slice of what constitutes "normal," then the boundaries tend to be more tightly held. (In polling about immigration, the areas with the strongest anti-immigrant views are those with the fewest immigrants!)

We fear what we don't know and fill in the gaps with our own imagination. I live in a village of seven hundred people in rural Southwest France. When we moved there in 2005 to establish our meditation center, my wife and children arrived in three flavors of exotic: brown-skinned, Buddhist, and British. People saw us through the lens of a certain suspicion, born mostly of unfamiliarity with those "three Bs," but over time, with meeting other parents at the school gates, chatting in the boulangerie, participating in local events, human contact proved more powerful than prejudice.

Expanding your us-field needs to be a conscious practice, if you want to genuinely include all beings in your heart and consciousness. Here are three dimensions of that practice—solidarity, community, and love.

Solidarity with Life

Teaching meditation retreats, I'm often in an us-field that can look and feel very welcoming and inclusive to many people there. It is one of the beautiful things about a retreat—the openness, acceptance, and care in a silent field of shared solidarity of practice. But when I look around the meditation hall, I also notice who's *not there.* It's usually a pretty white scene, for example. When we inhabit situations where the ethnic mix of the wider population isn't well represented (or even *at all* represented), we at least need to ask ourselves why that is, as we explored in an earlier chapter. Despite whatever inclusive *ideal* you may have, you need to keep asking yourself whom you relate to and whom you don't, and why. Whom you identify with and whom you don't. Whom it is easy to love and whom you put out of your heart.

This can happen in simple, unconscious ways. Like the woman on retreat with me last year who arrived at a retreat center in the UK and was asked with a kind intention and a friendly tone if she was there alone or had come with her husband. She identifies as gay, and the query put her in a box into which she didn't fit.

Whichever side of a situation like that we find ourselves on . . . we can practice. There is rich inner work to be done in exploring the assumptions we make a based on our unconscious prejudices, particularly around ethnicity, sexuality, gender, class, and various other categories of identity that we either see or simply assume. And when we find ourselves judged, ignored, inaccurately labeled, dismissed, misunderstood, or marginalized, we can also notice any tendency toward righteousness or hatred that might arise. It might be hard to practice forgiveness sometimes, but then, if it weren't hard, it wouldn't need to be a practice! When you feel you have been excluded from someone else's heart or consideration, unseen or unvalued, this is the time when you really get to see how willing you are not to exclude anyone from your own heart—most especially the one who seems to have just done that to you.

In January 2015, I was teaching meditation in San Francisco when the Charlie Hebdo attack happened in Paris. It was shocking and saddening. I followed social media as Parisian friends first expressed their grief, then defiance, and then solidarity, using the hashtag *#IamCharlie*. (Solidarity hashtagging has since become common, with Facebook offering ready-to-use "solidarity banners," as when many of us turned our profile pictures rainbow-colored when the U.S. government finally established equal marriage rights.)

I spoke with my wife, who was home in France. She also felt in solidarity with the national tragedy. Yet, as a brown-skinned woman, she felt an equal solidarity with all the Muslim French people who were encountering verbal and physical abuse in the days following the attack. Solidarity feels good (we love a cozy "us-field," a feeling of solidarity with "my people"), but where do you make its borders?

#IamCharlie too, but I'm also all those Pakistani families who have been killed by U.S. drone attacks. And I'm also the two thousand people who were massacred in Nigeria by Boko Haram the day before

the Charlie Hebdo attack, which received little international news attention. Why? Because they were outside the us-field. TV and press news are nation-centric, then ethnocentric. When French people get killed, the French press gets outraged. When African people get killed, it is still a human tragedy, but somehow it's seen as someone else's.

A relational practice asks each of us to confront where our human solidarity begins and ends. We *need* to evolve, collectively, to take *everyone* into our hearts. That opening is uncomfortable and vulnerable, but sometimes discomfort is important and necessary. Sometimes it is more important to be open than to be comfortable—more important to question and wrestle with the heart than to keep its boundaries closed.

Community: "As-One-ity"

The Buddha talked about the Three Jewels of this practice being Buddha, Dharma, Sangha. *Buddha* means awakening—the gradual and sudden extraordinary awakening to the way things are. *Dharma* means the nature of things, and the teachings that support that practice. And then, *Sangha* is—oh, other people! As a European, I've grown up in an intensely individualistic culture, where we value space and privacy and personal autonomy—where all the focus is on the individual's rights and freedoms. It is most explicitly enshrined by the delusional American Dream that you can be whatever you want to be—a neoliberal truism that ignores the systemic prejudice, marginalization, and oppression faced by some sections of the population.

Different cultures have different relationships to *comm-unity* (literally "as-one-ness") with other human beings. Where U.S. and European cultures emphasize individualistic identity, many other cultures are more collective—the primary identity established in relationship to belonging—a felt sense of identifying with the community more than with the individual. My Indian friend Wakhil, from Varanasi, was invited on a South Indian pilgrimage. His one condition for the journey was that he must not under any circumstances have to sleep alone. He told me, "I'll go on that journey as long as they don't give me a single room. My whole life, I've slept next to my brothers, uncles, and other family members. How miserable, lonely, and frightening to sleep in a room on my own." At Moulin de Chaves though, the meditation center in France where I live and teach, back in the realms of individuality, people will often only feel able to come on retreat if they can be sure of their own room. Sharing a room for some is a deal-breaker. "No single room? No retreat!"

Our individuality comes at a cost. While it fosters important qualities like confidence, agency, and independence, it also generates insecurity and alienation. I remember sitting in an empty train station waiting room, late at night in Delhi. After some time a man came in, and glancing around at all the empty seats, came straight over to sit right next to me. It was the obvious thing to do. In contrast, in European and American waiting rooms, people generally sit *as far away as possible* from the next, dreaded human being. It is partly out of respect for the other individual (let's keep that bit!), but also partly that our individualistic culture breeds a certain wariness, anxiety, and distrust of other human beings. And that bit we need to grow out of.

We *need* community—each other, warm bodies. Studies are increasingly telling us how addiction, depression, and anxiety disorders are deeply related to a lack of connection (as if we didn't know). Living alone, some people go weeks without simple, physical skin contact with another human—without a hug.

The COVID-19 pandemic (which had not begun at the time of writing, but now as I edit has become the defining feature of current times) has shown us the danger of hyperindividualism. Loud voices of objection to masks, social distancing, and sheltering at home are often much more focused on *my rights* as an individual than on *our responsibility* to take care of each other.

Yet contact can also feel threatening or invasive. For some people, one of the attractions of silent retreat is that you don't have to talk to anybody! And some of us by nature are just more introvert.

We just *like* being alone. Nevertheless, we live in a relational world, and one that is forcing us closer together. With the increasing risk of rising sea levels displacing populations, and as increasing temperature extremes compromise crowd yields and food availability, how will we manage if we gravitate toward conflict instead of collaboration, toward withdrawal instead of contact, toward individual greed instead of communal need?

Meditative experiences can take us into profound experiences of intimacy and belonging. Deep inter-being with the whole universe can be known in a breath or a sunset, but how easily that expansion shrinks back to self-conscious identification when you open your eyes and see *other human beings!* Our practice invites us to see where we shrink—and why.

We have to *build* community, both where we live and in *how* we live with each other. Perhaps the following reflections, and others like them, will become *life-saving* practices during the next few decades of ecological upheaval and societal transformation:

- How can you be with others and stay embodied?
- How can you stay in relationship when you disagree with your lover, colleague, or neighbor?
- How can you listen to the humanity of your family member, even when you disagree with their point of view?
- How can you contribute to the welfare and safety and ease of those around you?
- How can you strengthen bonds of care, empathy, and mutual support?

We can recognize several basic tendencies, all based on fear, in our contact with other humans. They arise from a fear of being ignored, a fear of being rejected, and a fear of being seen, and they correspond to the "three poisons" in Buddhist psychology—demanding, defensive, and deluded, respectively. One maladaptive tendency *demands* contact, in the form of attention. Another *defends* against contact, which feels intrusive. And a third *deludes* themselves about contact and the nature or intentions of the other.

If we use the microscope of meditative attention to zoom in on these tendencies, you can see which style you most recognize from your own relational patterns:

A demanding relational style is where you lean out of yourself into the other, trying to be pleasing, or to impress, or with a lot of anxious anticipation about what the other might be thinking about you. You feel dependent on the other's approval or appreciation, without which you feel inadequate or insecure. It can present as arrogance or as neediness, depending on what you are trying to get from or impress upon the other. Basically though, the neurotic is always checking: "Do you love me?"

The defending style occurs when you withdraw into yourself as a form of protection, an attempt to be self-reliant, independent, and invulnerable. Others may seem complicated or threatening, unreliable or untrustworthy, depending on your personality development and previous conditioning. This stance signifies "I don't need anyone."

"Deluded" relating is harder to pin down. You might flip from engagement to withdrawal, from being enamored of others to feeling betrayed by them. This personality often feels easily slighted or misunderstood. Their mantra might be: "You don't know me!"

Which of these three types do you recognize? Getting to know your own relating style is an important part of exploring it and getting free of it. Do you tend to withdraw, for example? If so, you can't just switch that off, but you can stay curious: *What am I withdrawing from? What might I be afraid of? Do I need to withdraw quite this much?* It's not that the answer is definitely no. If you have a lifelong pattern of withdrawal, then pulling back from others might feel very safe and necessary. But what might happen if you soften a little? Come forward a little, inhabit your body and feelings, just a little?

Or, if the tendency is to go out, then you can also explore: *What happens if I come back to myself? What is happening in my body while I'm fixating on the other person?* There is a certain irony in that we lean out of ourselves in an attempt to make contact, a quest for intimacy and connection—but actually the more we stay at home in ourselves, the more we are present for the actual experience of intimacy with another. Because, ultimately, *all* intimacy happens *here*, in your embodied experience. As soon as you lean out to please or impress the other, you make the other, well, *other*. The more you stay at home in your felt experience, whether you're agreeing with or arguing with someone, there's an intimacy possible, because where is that other? Oh, they're here. Here in awareness, here in the perception, the feeling, the contact. When you meet a so-called other in the actual recognition that the meeting is happening here, then you actually commune *as one*. This is the foundation of real community, and it's available with anyone. Everyone. Always. Whether they are able to commune with you or not.

Human beings are amazing, all of them. All of *us*. Deserving of our interest, deserving of our care, our solidarity, our understanding. Some actions are hard to understand. Some *actions* are impossible to be in solidarity with. But every heart feels the same basic experience as this heart—pain, confusion, struggle, joy. Every heart is longing for ease. Seeing this, we see our human community. It's not really even about my heart and your heart, my feelings or your feelings. We have *human* feelings, human life, a human body and heart and mind.

We've never been more aware as a species of how closely we live together, sharing the air and water and land of one planet. Pollution doesn't respect national borders. Trees act as the lungs of the whole planet, no matter where their location And the COVID-19 situation has made all too clear how interconnected we inevitably are. Yet this awareness of our fundamental nonseparation is too much for some, and they withdraw unconsciously into xenophobic tribalism, with the blame, persecution, and hatred that we see playing out so depressingly and dangerously in our politically and socially fractured world. For the sake of our human community and our deep solidarity with all of life, we all need to expand our view and our heart. And our opportunity is here, with the people around you, right now.

ALL YOU NEED IS . . .

When I despair, I remember that all through
history the way of truth and love have
always won. There have been tyrants and
murderers, and for a time they can seem
invincible, but in the end they always fall.
Think of it . . . always.

—MAHATMA GANDHI

Love is what we need. All of us. Love is the heart of relationship. Love dissolves division, whether between people or in your own heart. Love your own dark thoughts and they will cease to be monsters. Attend kindly to one who dislikes and disagrees with you, and you not only stop feeding their reactivity, you also melt your own. But this love is not something fluffy and lovey and *nice*. It is an intense practice, to love what is, whether you like it or not—and to love the one in front of you, whether you agree with them or not.

It is hard to speak of love without invoking romance. And I have nothing against romance—but unfortunately, it seems to have sucked up *all* the love. All the pop songs, valentine cards, rom-coms, and happily-ever-after fairy tales have put romantic love so center stage for us culturally, there's not much room left for the other deep features of the human heart. Love is the guide, the medicine, the very essence of relationship, but you can't get into *romantic* love with *everyone*, so we need another map for the territory of the heart—one that shows different nuances of love and directs our hearts toward them.

The Greeks had one such map, discerning six qualities of love: *Philia* is friendship, affectionate regard, platonic or "brotherly" love. *Eros* is romantic love, sexual passion. (Plato also included being attracted to the specific beauty of someone in *eros*, regardless of whether sexual passion is involved). *Agape* is the love for God and the love *of* God—selfless, altruistic love. *Storge* means "empathy, tenderness"—nurturing love—the love of parents for their children. *Pragma* is the steady, deep love that can develop over a long partnership or marriage. And *philautia* is self-love—a kind regard toward oneself—holding oneself with esteem.

These nuances, however, remain dualistic. The Greeks' varieties of love are given and received—there is subject and object. In contrast, as we'll see next, Buddha explored the heart qualities as *boundless* or *divine* abodes of the heart—qualities that dissolve all boundaries, but most specifically those of giver and receiver. When the heart is truly expanded, you cannot say if you are the lover or the beloved—you don't feel yourself as the subject, the *source* of love, but instead that the giver and receiver exist *in love.* As love.

All is love, the spiritual platitude tells us, but how can all be love when there is so much hatred, confusion, and tragedy? And how can you meaningfully *practice* this love?

The infinite stretches of the heart deserve their own open space, so we'll turn heartward now.

7

This Body of Love

FOUR FLAVORS OF LOVE

If you're familiar with Buddhist practice, you'll probably know these four Pali terms—*metta, karuna, mudita,* and *upekkha*—and probably their English translations as loving-kindness, compassion, appreciative joy, and equanimity. As we explore them, I'll use slightly different terms for them and we'll look at several features:

- *The nuance of love:* How the particular heart quality meets experience
- *The boundless quality:* The way the heart expands, opens . . . loves
- *The universal felt sense:* How the heart experiences this form of love, physically and energetically
- *The transformational quality:* What specifically gets liberated, and what happens typically to the heart, and life, without this quality

We'll explore these concepts one by one. We'll see how each quality arises as the heart's response to a specific kind of experience. The qualities can be intentionally cultivated in various ways, but most fundamentally they express the inherent nature of the free heart.

Four Flavors of Love: A Map of the Liberated Heart

Pali name	Nuance of love	Boundless quality	Felt sense	Transformation
Metta	**The love that cares** Care—goodwill—friendliness	**Boundless friendliness** The default resting place of the free heart, that stays fundamentally open toward, and well-disposed toward whatever or whoever appears	**The radiant heart** Experienced as a warmth in the heart-center that you can feel radiating, expanding, spreading outward	**Antidote to pettiness** The more you care, the less you get caught in useless or petty drama and detail
Karuna	**The love that responds** Compassion, the solidarity of the heart with suffering	**Boundless compassion** The free heart's response to life's inevitable pain and loss	**An undefended heart** Experienced as an ache in the heart, a kind of heartbreak: the pain of the heart breaking open in solidarity with suffering—whether one's own or anyone else's	**Antidote to judgment** The more one recognizes and feels the truth of painful experience, the less judgmental or harsh one is. One learns how to cry true tears and to reach out and help, as a neutral expression of love.
Mudita	**The love that delights** Joy, delight, pleasure, gratitude, wonder, appreciation	**Boundless joy** The free heart's capacity to delight and wonder at all that is beautiful	**Champagne in the heart** Experienced as a fizzing in the chest center, like the fine bubbles of champagne. Exuberance, delight, bliss. Happiness that there is joy and beauty in life.	**Antidote to consumptive gratification** When you are nourished by real joy and delight, you are less dependent on coarser pleasures, less needy of gratification, less dependent on getting what you want.

Upekkha	The love that allows	Boundless space	A wide-open heart	Antidote to a diminishing comfort zone
	Spaciousness, peace, openness, nonreactivity, equanimity	The openness of the free heart that can open to and include all that arises, whether agreeable or disagreeable, pleasurable or painful	Experienced as space, openness, the feeling in the chest of naturally making room for whatever appears. The heart feels vast, spacious, able to embrace experience of whatever type.	Wide-open heart feels naturally patient. One is gracious and spacious in the face of discomfort— increasingly able to freely abide, whether comfortable or not.

METTA—THE LOVE THAT CARES

To *care* is to feel a basic goodwill, a friendliness, toward life. It is the radiant warmth of heart that we all know in those moments of feeling simply, kindly disposed toward someone. One wishes them well. Without qualifiers or conditions. One wants them to be content and at ease, to enjoy good fortune and to be safe from harm.

These are the kinds of phrases that make up formal *metta* practice, where one directs caring wishes toward oneself, others, and all beings. This practice has become something of an orthodoxy in the Western Buddhist meditation scene over the last few decades. Originally though, all four of the boundless qualities were considered not as practices but simply as orientations of the heart. The encouragement was to abide, *radiating kindness over the entire world*, taking experience into one's heart in a caring embrace like a mother's love, as in this passage from Karaniya Metta Sutta, translated by the Amaravati Sangha (https://www.accesstoinsight.org/tipitaka/kn/khp/khp.9.amar.html):

> Even as a mother protects with her life, her
>   child, her only child,
> So with a boundless heart one cherishes all
>   living beings;

Radiating kindness over the entire world:
Spreading upwards to the skies,
    And downwards to the depths—
Outwards and unbounded,
    Freed from hatred and ill-will.

I used to teach a retreat at a convent about an hour south of Paris, the Prieuré St. Thomas. There is a beautiful polished wooden statue there of the classic image of Mary holding the baby Jesus. In this particular statue, there is a feeling of incredible tenderness, a mother bathing her son in the love of her maternal gaze. The statue must have been carved by someone who had a real feel for the quality of heart represented by the image. If people were having a hard time in the retreat, and particularly if they were giving *themselves* a hard time, I would send them to sit awhile with this statue, encouraging them to turn that same tender gaze toward their own experience.

That is what *metta* feels like. No matter where it is directed, it is warm and well-wishing. We all know the experience of care, but usually within certain parameters (the boundaries of our us-field)—children, family, loved ones (for some, animals are easier to be with than other humans, and it is pets that give the easiest access).

Freeing the heart points us toward an infinite capacity to care. This is actually the default setting, the natural resting place or a genuinely free heart. The love of an essentially benevolent gaze is the way the free heart looks out at life. It is nontransactional, nonreward seeking, because love is its only reward. There is no more gratifying state than to love. It gives a great buoyancy, a taste of fulfillment, a sense that all is lovable and that in opening the heart to all, one is also held oneself within that infinite embrace. It is the sense that nobody is, that nobody even *could be*, excluded from the embrace of my heart.

The essential felt sense of this benevolence is a warm radiance in the heart. It feels physically not dissimilar to the way a medicinal brandy warms the inside of the chest, though it is subtler and finer, and accompanied by that radiance.

Benevolence literally means "well-wishing." It is the natural extension of that radiance toward whoever enters our experience. Self or other, friend or stranger. Not about whether it goes outward or inward, to the one we call "self" or "other," but rather about the experience of the heart having a benevolent atmosphere. Whatever appears is welcomed, honored, allowed to pass through gracefully and graciously.

Why Is It Hard to Care?

We all long to love and be loved. We know that caring, whether for ourselves or others, soothes the heart. We paste reassuring quotes about love on social media, over backgrounds of mountains and oceans that suggest the great expansive beauty of love. So how come it is so difficult sometimes? How come the doors of the heart keep clanging shut, pulling us back into the protective, competitive battle of self versus the world? First, because the habit of self-absorption is really strong. It looks as if there is a whole universe out there, and I am somehow separate from it. And to the extent we keep reinforcing self-separation through our perception, thought, and sense of identity, then *my* needs, *my* wants, *my* safety, *my* issues, *my* problems, and *my* life just soak up all the heart-space. My oh my!

Then there are also the imprints of your personal history—the beliefs we each carry—until they are really explored and resolved—that tell us we are somehow fundamentally unlovable—that people will leave me / criticize me / ignore me / hurt me / abuse me. That is why the wounds of childhood—particularly if they run to the extremes of neglect, violence, and abuse—are so pernicious and their effects often so devastating. Their imprints have obscured our trust in our own heart, which needs to be explored and untangled. Love is the fruit of this disentangling, and it is also a way into the defended heart, turning toward one's own pain the way Mary turns toward Jesus in the polished wooden statue described earlier.

It can feel as if it might be just too much to really care. As if, were I to really allow the whole world into my heart, I would somehow lose myself, swallowed up in this ocean of all-encompassing care. And that is true, in a way. Love is powerful, and in the first moments when the vast radiance of the heart is really felt, it can be overwhelming, even frightening, as we can feel we are losing ourselves, losing our usual reference points, losing our self-security, swamped by love like an island in rising floodwaters. We are so used to self-concern that we get disoriented by its absence, afraid of this great openheartedness. To practice care is to familiarize ourselves with this expansiveness, this radiance of heart, so we can stabilize in it. Just as we explored earlier the natural progression from ego-centric through group-centric to world-centric, as we get familiar with the tender heart, as we allow our old defenses to drop and melt, we move naturally from ego-centric care as something "I am doing" to a liberated vision of care where neither loving nor being loved is mine, but rather the inherent nature of the free heart.

Everyone Is Trying Their Best

> We're all just walking each other home.
>
> —RAM DASS

Buddhist psychology views humans as being "made of" basic goodness. Nobody wants to be an asshole. Everyone is trying to get their needs met and hoping to get loved and valued by others along the way. Yet each person's attempts are filtered through the fog of their own patterning. Think how much you are driven by your own desires, fears, and habits. If you see others behaving in ways you wouldn't approve of, can you not see at least the seeds of those same kinds of beliefs and behaviors in your own mind, even if they are smaller in scale? If I were to expand on Ram Dass's line from above, I'd say:

> We're all trying our best.
> We're all constantly messing up.
> We're all walking each other home.

Personally I have seen all kinds of judgmental, mean-spirited, petty, cruel, and intolerant impulses flicker through my awareness. But I don't take them personally. I don't make a problem out of them and I don't entertain them. (Like Suzuki Roshi says of attending to the mind, "Leave your front door and your back door open. Let thoughts come and go. Just don't serve them tea.") Crucially, I also don't imagine that I, or anyone else, shouldn't have those thoughts. My shorthand for what I can reasonably expect of my mind is that it is often needy, greedy, lazy, and crazy. This way, I am neither surprised nor alarmed by my own thoughts as I watch them pass through, doing their own needy, greedy thing.

A truly expansive heart is distinct from merely "feeling loving" toward a person, place, or thing. We often use the term *love* to mean "like very much" or "experience strongly pleasant sensations in connection with." "I love chocolate," we say, or "I love going to concerts." Or "I love you," even. When we say that last one, we would like to think we mean that I care for you, that I'll support and nourish and nurture you, that I'll be here for you through the proverbial "better and worse, richer and poorer." It is interesting to note, though, when the impulse to utter those iconic three words springs to our lips. Often it is simply in response to pleasure and gratification. You do or say something I like, and ta-dah, "I love you!"

Self-Care

Be kind to yourself. Kindness is relaxing, and there is no way you can settle deeply into your experience if you are berating, blaming, or beating up on yourself. You can see the painful, tragic consequences for those who don't get very far in developing this quality. They get petty, mean-spirited, and grumpy. As you age, your patterns get stronger ("whatever you feed, that's what grows"), and if it is not love that feeds your heart, then inevitably it will be its opposite. If your heart can't give itself up into caring and kindness, it will be left in the prison of suspicion and grump.

It is a popular spiritual cliché that you cannot really love another if you don't love yourself. Many of us, however, are quite good at attending gently and generously to others' needs, yet become harsh and self-forgetting when it comes to real self-care. Your heart has borne all kinds of hurts and disappointments, losses and betrayals, through all the years of your life. I promise you, that you long deeply, more than you know, and that you deserve deeply, whatever your story, to be held gently by your own heart. Most of us have become so used to a kind of half-defended, half-distracted relationship to our inner experience that we don't know what it feels like to really care for ourselves. We compensate in all kinds of unsatisfactory ways, but there is no real substitute for genuine self-care.

I'm often on the road, teaching and traveling—sleeping alone, eating alone. Walking into a restaurant for yet another "Dinner for one" is fertile ground for boredom and loneliness to appear. And those conditions, which at first sound miserable, make for a very good invitation for self-care. They invite me to accompany myself, to hold myself, to be my own friend—the one who listens deeply to me. Staying alone in a hotel room invites me to care for myself in a different way from being at home. That dinner for one is an invitation to be my own guest! To feed myself like Mary would have fed Jesus. Please try this for yourself next time you are feeling lonely, bored, or abandoned. Find out what lovely company you can be!

In this way, loneliness is a gateway to intimacy. Turning toward the lonely feeling shows that in fact you are not alone. If loneliness can be met and held by awareness, then you are not lonely. You are held, and you are holding. This is a powerful way to undo the pernicious habit of nearly everyone: giving yourself a hard time. Anyone who lives fundamentally at ease with themselves has abandoned this toxic habit. It doesn't mean you never have remorse or make a mistake that you feel badly about. It means you don't blame and berate yourself. You can evaluate your actions and make amends if you have made a mistake, but you no longer *judge* yourself. This is the difference between *remorse* and *guilt*. The former is useful: *Let me look back, and if I spoke or acted unwisely or unkindly, let me learn from that.* The latter, however, is just a self-attack, an excuse for giving yourself a hard time. Which, as we saw in great detail in an earlier chapter, is never useful. Genuine care, gentleness of heart, is the ultimate antidote to judgment, as exemplified by Jesus, bleeding from his sword-cut ear and being dragged to prison: "Forgive them—they know not what they do."

Practicing Metta

Plenty of good material has been written about the formal metta practices of repeating well-wishing phrases, directed inwardly and outwardly, so I won't focus on them here—partly because others have done so already and partly because they've not been an avenue of practice for me. I know many who have benefited greatly from phrase repetition, but personally I have always gravitated more to the *feeling of* benevolence rather than to a *formula for* generating it. Care is an inherent quality of awareness. If you want your experience to open up, meet it kindly. Allow the heart's natural loving wish to have enough air and exposure that it grows naturally, until it is an obvious part of your functioning, a natural resting place of the heart. Here are a couple of informal ways you might tilt your heart in that direction:

Start with whomever you find it easy to love—dear friends, children, or pets. Love them, which is easy and natural anyway, and *feel the natural expansion of your heart.* Feel the cognac warmth that spreads in your chest. Feel the love that loves, that loves to love. Imagine how that could expand, and see if you can dare to let it. You might find you have a greater capacity for caring than you ever imagined.

There is no behavior, no reaction, no judgment, or prejudice, or violent action I've seen for which I cannot recognize the same impulse, however scaled-down or fleeting it may have been, in my own consciousness. And whatever hope for love or wish for safety and comfort I have known, I can be absolutely certain that others share these same wishes. In other words, this world of humans and creatures are *just like me.* Just like you. When you find you have put others out of your heart—no doubt for some "good reason"—what is it like to consider that this person, "this fool, this enemy, this wrong-headed idiot" is, in fact, *just like me.* Emphasize the similarities rather than the differences. It will make you feel closer to all these so-called others. In this way, we care for all the world.

But what is the world? It is the realm of experience—the whole gestalt of what we call *self, other, and environment,* all inseparable. And it is possible to know a deep friendliness for all of it. You can have a love affair with the world, you can care for trees, be loved by the earth as you lie flat on her ground, be embraced by darkness, and caressed by wind. Without this deep, delicious intimacy with life, the heart closes around petty self-interest, but where does "the world" end and the abstraction of it become created in your mind? Can you separate yourself from the world, or are self and world always and irrevocably intimate with each other? Bound up inseparably. You are the world—the whole universe, quite literally. Knowing this in the marrow of your being is where true care comes from—effortlessly, naturally, unstoppably.

Karuna: The Love That Responds

Compassion, from its Latin root, literally means "to suffer with," that is, to be in solidarity with suffering—to tend to it, respond to it, seek to relieve it—this is love in action.

Compassion is the love that responds, the love that does not turn away, the love that tends to pain, the love that opens to suffering.

It is hard to love that which is painful. We either want to turn away because it hurts or to shut down to protect ourselves, or we can feel overwhelmed by sorrow or fear or our incapacity to make it all better. Yet the best way to be psychologically prepared to meet and respond to the inevitable pain, loss, heartbreak, and grief that we all experience is actually to lean into it. We learn to tend to that which is painful, because the tending itself is soothing. Liberating. It is love.

Turning toward Pain

To make that turn toward, you don't need to wait for some difficult circumstance to befall either you or someone close to you. There is pain and dissatisfaction, frustration and fear enough in the moments of any day to cultivate a tender relationship with the unwelcome and unwanted. The practice of compassion is, in great measure, befriending and tending to the inevitable loneliness and fear, agitation and insecurity, confusion and despair that assail us all at times. These difficult places in the heart are purified and transformed through direct contact, curiosity, and care.

Think about your daily life—every day confronted by at least some physical discomfort, emotional disappointment, and mental agitation. We easily see these as annoyances to be rid of, but they are actually the training wheels of our capacity to be with any and *all* pain. In his *Divine Comedy*, Dante's sign above the entrance to Hell reads "Abandon All Hope You Who Enter Here." Rather than a message of hopelessness, as it may first appear, this initially daunting phrase is actually the "survival instructions" for passing through hellish conditions: Abandon your obsessive, angsty thinking about how things could or should be different, worrying about who is to blame and generating endless self-pity. Then you can actually meet and manage *the way things are right now*. Winston Churchill in his deadpan fashion, famously offered a similar encouragement: "When you're going through hell, keep going."

How does a free heart experience and respond to suffering? By feeling it—fully. By not turning away and not shutting down. The universal felt sense of compassion is as a deep, painful ache in the heart. It hurts. But after a lifetime of turning away or shutting down, what are you going to do? You turn, gently, just a little at first, maybe—you turn toward it. You let it in. You let your heart break. Which feels unmanageable on the way in, until you realize that it is breaking . . . open. This is actually the remedy for the defended heart. The pain of life—yours, mine, or the whole shebang—seems too much if you are trying to contain it in just your own poor little emotional chest-container. But really let it in, and it will transform you. It will give you courage and tenderness and the capacity to respond, to speak and act in service of the free heart's natural wish. Just as when stubbing your toe, your hand reaches out naturally to soothe it, so a free heart reaches out to tend to wherever there is pain.

We have plenty of inspiring exemplars: Nelson Mandela and the Dalai Lama are perhaps the most obvious—men who have stood up to violence and persecution with great goodness of heart. But don't overlook more recent examples (and don't let men take all the limelight!)

Malala Yousafzai has shown incredible heart in her tireless advocacy for girls' education. She was shot in the head in 2012, in an assassination attempt by the Pakistani Taliban, and has brought her loving and fearless work to international attention since.

Emma Gonzalez metabolized the tragedy of the mass shooting at her high school in Florida in 2018 to become a vocal campaigner and activist for gun control in the United States. You have only to hear a small piece of these young women's stories, or watch them for a moment on TV, to see how pain and suffering can be powerfully transformed by the heart into love. Fierce, courageous, unflinching, clear-sighted love, boundless love.

That love is the love that allows Malala to speak and act and forgive her enemies; that lets Emma continue her work in the face of racial abuse, hate speech, and death threats; that gave Tibetan nuns the capacity to forgive their Chinese jailers after being imprisoned and relentlessly tortured for simply reciting their prayers, saying their greatest fear in prison was that they might lose their compassion for their jailers.

If you want to tend to pain, you cannot get stuck on blame and righteousness and victimhood. The unfortunate, the unwelcome, the unjust, and the unjustifiable can arrive at any moment. What will you do when it knocks on your door—when it enters your heart?

Tears of Compassion—Death and Grief

While traveling in Asia some years ago, American Dharma teacher Larry Rosenberg had the opportunity to attend the funerals of two Buddhist monks in different traditions. At the first, in Korea, he sat next to a monk who wept at his loss. "I entered the monastery the same day as he who has died. He was my closest Dharma brother and I will miss him greatly," he said. Sometime later at the funeral of a monk in Thailand, Larry sat next to another monk, who sat stoically and steadily, grounded in the truth of impermanence, awake to the truth that all must die.

Which is the wiser response? The clearer, the deeper, the truer way to meet death? (It's OK not to know—it's a trick question). There's no "right" way to grieve. As the first monk expressed, it is poignant to lose one we love. As the second showed, this is the natural fate of all of us, and if we are awake to that, we can honor and remember the loved one without losing our ground.

For myself, when someone I have known and cared for dies, most of what I feel is love. Love and poignancy and mystery. Love that arises as sorrow, and as missing the person, and as delight for who they were, and as perplexity at the mystery of whatever has happened to them now. All that lives, dies, and we don't get to control the circumstances or the timing. Fundamentally, there is no tragedy in death, though it can be painful for the bereaved, trying to manage the pain of loss, confusion, and hurt.

For some, grief is intense and all consuming for a while. For others it comes and goes in waves, and for others still it smolders in the background, never quite bursting into flame, nor ever quite going out. As I say, there is no right way to grieve. What is helpful, though, is to give most of your attention to the feelings, not the story. Let yourself feel the love and loss, and don't dwell on the why and how and if and but of the beloved's passing. Grief is born of love. Recognize that you love the person. Talk to them if you want. Say what was left unsaid. Honor the relationship. Take the time to get comfortable with the unfathomableness of losing someone and not having any kind of ready answer as to what has become of them.

The Clarity of Suffering

Suffering can also quiet and focus the mind. In the midst of a sudden challenge or calamity, we forget the extraneous, the facile, the superficial. It is common in cancer patients, or others with a terminal illness, to discover newfound clarity and dignity in the sudden focus on the essential, the immediate, the *right here.* There is a certain freedom of heart available right in the midst of the painful, like a beautiful lotus growing out of the muck of unwished for circumstances.

When I was first in the Himalayas, aged nineteen, I rented a small, cold hut in Dharamsala. I had arrived with dysentery, and for a couple of weeks I was weak, in pain, and delirious, whilst shitting and vomiting my guts out. I would often wake to find I'd soiled the bed and would have to walk down the street to the public tap to wash out my *lunghi* (a robe worn around the waist like a sarong) and sheets before swaying, exhausted, back to bed. After about ten days of this, my mind would come up with all kind of doubtful thoughts. Am I dying? Will I ever get better? In my delirium I really didn't know how close I might be to death, nor what I could do about my situation. But having recently discovered and embraced Dharma practice, I was very close to my experience. I watched the waves of fear arise and pass. I saw thoughts of self-pity and panic come and go. Yet amid all of that was a kind of crystalline clarity:

> I am here. My heart is intact. I don't want to die but I also don't want to fight. And I feel like I am just where I should be. I would love to feel better, but I don't want to fight with the way life is right now. My freedom and ease of being are contingent not on my fantasy of how the situation could or should improve, but on my capacity to meet this moment. To care for this breath, to wash these sheets, to shit and shiver as graciously and spaciously as possible.

It was a deeply unpleasant time, but I tasted a profoundly important sense of freedom in that experience. It is my own reactivity, not illness and misfortune, that is the real enemy of my ease and well-being.

All of that might seem a bit passive. One might ask: *Why didn't you go see a doctor, you idiot?* That's a good question. My newfound willingness to be with my experience was a bit out of balance with a more pragmatic wisdom. But that experience deeply shaped me and contributed to a certain fearlessness around misfortune, illness, calamity, and death. I am deeply thankful to that nineteen-year-old's idealism and his youthful zeal for practice.

The essence of compassion is in the response we make to whatever is painful. A fearless heart responds, though we cannot anticipate how. Sometimes it is by standing up and speaking out, like Emma Gonzalez. At other times there is nothing we can do *except* (and this is also a crucially important response) letting the pain enter. Letting ourselves know the heart that feels and yet is undaunted. Turning toward suffering—even when there is nothing concrete we can do in response—readies the heart for the times when we *can* do something.

We have a massive challenge coming at us. All of us. Climate disruption, rising sea levels, and population displacement are bearing down on us. Violent conflict over food scarcity, freshwater availability, and ever-dwindling natural resources will also exert their pressures in the years and decades to come. I have no idea how those things will play out, but I do know you will *need* a resilient, wide-open heart if you want to live fully in the midst of that. And die freely when the time comes.

Bullshit in Compassion Drag

If you are orienting toward a true, radical freedom of the heart, then you also have to navigate the many bullshit responses to suffering, modeled to us in popular culture. We see politicians making cuts to social welfare spending, failing to deal with homelessness, inequality, racism, and the climate emergency—showing moral outrage when the issue aligns with political or economic objectives and turning a cold, blind eye when it doesn't. The tired old "thoughts and prayers" offered instead of actual policy change to victims of mass shootings are phrased in a way to sound compassionate, yet without any actual response. Spouting compassionate platitudes, without doing what we can to actually make a difference, is what my teacher called "idiot compassion"—or bullshit in compassion drag.

Pain in the Family

What is your style when confronted with the painful? Do you tend toward shutting down, being overwhelmed, or getting distracted? We have some biological conditioning around protecting ourselves from pain, as we saw in the chapter on the instincts. These are further compounded by cultural imprints—the manipulative marketing machine that suggests life can be limitlessly comfortable and easy. And then our family imprints add another layer.

How was pain met in your family? Did you have one or more parents who was particularly cold-hearted. Or smothering? Or overly anxious about their children getting hurt? Reflect on what you picked up in your family of origin, and you may find important links to your relationship now to discomfort, disease, disturbance, and disaster.

What happened when there was a death, for example, or a serious illness in your family? Sometimes we "don't tell the children," in a misguided attempt to protect their emotional life that can end up feeling like a betrayal of trust and honesty. For others there is too much attention to pain. Some parents, unskilled in being with discomfort themselves, then act that out with their children, catastrophizing when the child falls over, smothering the child's feelings so they have no room to process pain by themselves: "Oh, you poor darling. What a horrible thing to happen. Let me give you some candy to help it feel better and then we'll get a big bandage on that little graze."

Other habits of emotional avoidance include denial of pain, classically employed when a child is hurt: "Oh it's nothing. Don't cry. Big girls/boys don't cry. Come on, pull yourself together." Or, teaching the child to project blame outward for any pain that arises: "Bad tree! Stupid tree, why did it have its branch hanging down like that when you were walking past?"

If you want to avoid giving these confusing and unhelpful signals to the children in your life, try describing the situation as you see it and actually finding out how they are coping with it:

"That looked painful, how are you feeling?"

"I can see your knee has turned red. Is it painful?"

"That sounded like a hard fall. What do you need?"

In short, whether with children or adults, the same basic guideline applies: Honor the other's experience, while giving them the space to do their own processing.

Practicing with Discomfort

If you don't train your capacity to tolerate the unwelcome and the uncomfortable, if you can't tend gently and compassionately to sorrow and grief and unpleasantness, then you'll end up with the opposite. Yes, *whatever you feed, that's what grows.* Look at people who have not done that work, and you'll see that as they age, they get more judgmental. More intolerant. The defended heart's tendency to shut down or turn away grows stronger, and magically, with all the social consequences we see around us, it becomes easier to dismiss the homeless or the refugee, the poor and the needy. It becomes easier to put people out of your heart.

Meditation, in many ways, is a powerful training in abiding with the uncomfortable. To sit still with yourself is to confront your creaky body and uncooperative mind, and leaning in to discomfort is a powerful training in the fearlessness of the heart. A famous old Zen story tells how a samurai, trying to impress a Zen master, waved his sword in front of him and declared: "I am one who can cut off your head without blinking an eye." The master looked smilingly up at the saber-rattling samurai and replied gently: "And I am one who can have his head cut off without blinking an eye."

People often ask me how long or how much they should sit with discomfort. How long is a piece of string? It depends on what you are cultivating. There is great value in abiding with discomfort and leaning into it, but only if you are doing so in the service of being loving—*tending* to the discomfort. If you can do that, then please, keep sitting. And at the point when you can no longer do that, when your back is too sore and your legs are too stiff and your morale has gone, and you are just gritting your teeth and cultivating sheer *bloody-mindedness*, then at that point, *please*, stop. Take care of yourself. Meditation is not supposed to be a battle.

Find Ways to Respond

In your life as it is right now, where can you care? Whom can you serve? Whom might you reach out to, where your support might make a huge difference, and in the service of whom you offer the *love* that is the essence of compassionate action?

In 2002, a student called Tony came up to thank me at the end of a retreat in the UK. It had been life-changing, he said. He had felt the suffering in the world and wanted to make a difference. His sincerity and conviction struck me powerfully, so I remembered him when, six months later, he came on another retreat. This time he arrived in a camper van, telling me that since the last retreat he had sold his apartment, quit his job, left his girlfriend, and given away all his possessions. This was the beginning of his new life, and beyond the retreat it was destination unknown. He was on a mission to change the world, and he didn't know where to start except for doing another retreat.

I saw Tony a few times over the next few years, then heard that his wandering had brought him somewhat randomly to China, and that a chance encounter with a beggar had given rise to him starting China's first-ever soup kitchen. A bit hazy on the details,

I just googled him now to get the facts (Tony Day, Yellow River Soup Kitchen). Yellow River has had twelve thousand volunteers, served hundreds of thousands of meals to people in need, and run over two thousand different humanitarian projects. Tony basically just followed his compassionate heart. Without a plan, without a clear vision. But also without shutting down. Without detaching himself from the fierce heart's longing to be of service. Love in action—compassion.

Maybe that seems beyond your scope. But look around you. Increasingly inhuman public health and welfare cuts mean that there are growing numbers of homeless people in pretty much all major cities, and increasingly even in smaller towns. Your offering may not be a whole soup kitchen, but what about a single cup of soup for the next homeless person you pass? Or a pair of clean socks? Or some human conversation? When we open our yes and hearts, we can see that someone, just nearby, could really do with a bit of love. And this is our practice. Let the Buddhists *wish people* free of pain. Let us reach out and *help people* deal with the pain of life. Our hearts, yours, and mine, and all of ours, long to love and be loved.

MUDITA: THE LOVE THAT DELIGHTS

A free heart doesn't choose its orientation, it responds to whatever is present. Basic care, or metta, is the default setting of the heart, just as a compass will naturally and consistently swing to north by default. If there is any other magnetic influence, however, the needle will swing in that direction. If what appears in awareness is painful, the free heart will swing to compassion, or *karuna*. If what arises is sweet or beautiful, the response is naturally one of joy and appreciation. *Mudita* is this love, that opens to beauty—the heart's boundless capacity to enjoy. A free heart sees much to appreciate, and is easily nourished, uplifted, and delighted.

As this capacity develops and deepens, you see more and more to appreciate and delight in. You find more moments to enjoy, more reasons to be grateful, more and more evidence of life's beauty and bounty.

As fear and armoring dissolve, these inherent expressions of your heart's fundamentally loving nature are what you find. If metta is felt as a warm glow of benevolence in the heart, and compassion is the heart's ache of pain and empathy, then the way we feel delight is as a kind of bubbling joy—like champagne in the heart: golden, fizzing, celebratory.

There is always something to appreciate, even when circumstances are highly unfavorable or inconvenient. The Dalai Lama shows us this quality—his joy seems boundless and infectious, though he has spent much of his life dealing with the fallout from the Chinese oppression and genocide of his people. Etty Hellesum was another such exemplar. Writing a journal for the two years prior to her death in Auschwitz at twenty-two, amid hellish conditions she pointed again and again to the depth of the human spirit. "Despite everything," she wrote, "Life is full of depth and meaning." Her last note, thrown from the train carrying her to Auschwitz, describes this great lightness of heart, ending: "We left the camp singing." Two months later she was dead.

Earlier, I mentioned those two weeks of diarrhea and delirium that I sweated and shitted through in the Himalayas. As well as the weakness and fever, though, I also remember the light of the mornings, the mountain air, and the feeling that despite everything, there was really nowhere on earth I would rather be. As Leonard Cohen famously reminded us, "There is a crack, a crack in everything. That's how the light gets in."

Joy is sometimes of *most* use when things go wrong. We easily get caught in blame and drama, but the loss of familiar expectations can strip away our complacency. Coming home to find he had been robbed of all his possessions, the Japanese poet, monk, and vagabond Ryokan looks out of his empty hut at the night sky: "Poor fellow. How I wish I could have offered him this beautiful moon."

We lose what we love, inevitably. Sunshine turns to rain. Life is no respecter of our preferences. Yet here we are. Alive. Conscious. Breathing. Is it possible that you are floating, constantly, and most especially *right now*, in an ocean of blessings? Even if sometimes it feels like you are drowning?

The Blessings of Your Life

I had a friend in school who always had something to worry about: family, grades, girlfriends, fashion—*anything.* Then one sunny day, everything was weirdly fine and he couldn't find anything to worry about. And that made him really worried. He had the clarity to recognize this, and the honesty to tell me that "I'm worried that I have nothing to worry about." Perhaps you recognize this condition. Worry can be extremely seductive—having problems to solve gives you a sense of purpose, a focus upon which to hang your sense of self—a seemingly good reason to *take yourself seriously.* An old friend and I affectionately remind each other of this. When one of us gets a little too involved in the drama and detail of our lives, the other will reply, "Yes, I know, you're *very busy and important*!"

Though we dislike the agitation and uncertainty of worry, we are reluctant to give up feeling busy and important. But how might your life be transformed by abandoning habitual worry? How might your heart be transformed, if you reflected on the blessings of your own life?

I was teaching in London recently during some very cold weather. With so many visible signs of immense wealth and privilege in the city, it's easy to see those who appear to have more than us and to somehow feel deprived, but on this cold afternoon, we reflected on our capacity to go home and be warm—a luxury many don't have—and how some could even choose the exact temperature of heat in their homes. We considered our ability to clothe ourselves adequately for the weather—again, a luxury not shared by all—and even to be able to choose from several outfits for that. We continued with how we could take for granted that we would eat that evening—another privilege not afforded everyone—and how we might be able to choose between eating in or out, or between this or that kind of food.

Taking our everyday blessings for granted, we deprive ourselves of the openhearted appreciation that is mudita. *Counting your blessings* is a powerful way to cultivate this quality, whether in the popular practice of making some kind of gratitude list or simply reflecting on your good fortune. Our famous "negativity bias" will pull attention toward what's *wrong*—what you imagine could or should be better about you or your circumstances. What if you were to consciously direct your attention, again and again until it become an effortless habit, toward what's *right*? All that is well with you. All you have to appreciate. Whatever health and wealth you have, whatever clothing and shelter, whatever family and social support. Perhaps you will find a bottomless well of appreciation for the blessings of your life.

The Buoyant Heart

Our being has a fundamental buoyancy to it. The heart that knows its access to joy is irrepressible. Life's circumstances can submerge us, but no matter how hard you try to sink a buoy, it's nature is to right itself, resurface, and float. Only when the air is squeezed out does it sink, and until life squeezes the last breath from you, the nature of your heart is buoyant. The more you love and appreciate what is within and around you, the more you discover this essential buoyancy—the more you feel the fizzing delight champagne of a joyful heart.

The Theravada tradition in which I trained is not the best exemplar of celebration and joy. There is a certain beauty in the rhythms of chanting, the gilded buddhas, and offering ceremonies. But there is also the sense that delight somehow belongs to the territory of "sensual pleasure," which in a renunciant tradition is to be avoided. The term *mudita* was first clumsily translated as "sympathetic joy," suggesting a gladness only at the good fortune of others. Yet love dissolves distinctions. The free and joyous heart doesn't discriminate between your good fortune or mine. It delights in goodness and beauty, wherever it occurs.

Beauty is nourishing and draws awareness. Drink tea from a fine Japanese tea bowl and the delicacy of the ceramic naturally draws your attention and appreciation (as opposed to the all too British "tradition" of drinking tea from old, chipped, random mugs!). The Zen tradition understands this well. Calligraphy, flower arranging, gardening, and many otherwise quotidian expressions are suffused with a beauty of gesture. They remind us that just this moment, just this object, just this ordinary humanness of ours, is to be treasured, honored, and rejoiced in.

Honoring beauty is an invitation to the heart: Notice. Appreciate. Enjoy! This quality underpins the aesthetic decisions we make at the Moulin, because when you come on retreat with me I want you to delight in the place and feel the goodness of the environment, to relax into being here and feel *glad-hearted* about being on retreat.

The Repression of Joy

Many of us feel we somehow don't deserve to really be joyful. As a child, you may have been told to "calm down," to not get "overexcited," to not "show off" or be "too much." Internalizing that message, you may then feel self-conscious and uneasy about being unabashedly playful or joyful. If your natural exuberance was hushed, ridiculed, or shamed into submission, you may no longer know how to access it nor how it feels. Unresolved childhood unease and guilt around being exuberant can also produce ambivalent feelings about being joyful in a world where so many suffer. If joy doesn't come easily to you, look and see what beliefs you have about yourself. I remember, particularly at school, being told to "wipe that smile off your face," that "Life is not all fun and games, you know!" and that I needed to "take things more seriously." I learned that joy was frivolous and unwelcome, and had no place in being responsible and adult, and I've had to *relearn* the art of enjoying since.

Consider your own history:

Reflection

How much delight and joy, ease and celebration was present in your early life? What did you pick up in your family about attitudes to beauty, gratitude, blessing, fun? How did it affect you and may still be affecting you?

The Art of Enjoying

As with the other heart qualities, what you feed, grows. If you don't cultivate the free heart's deep capacity for joy, then you end up relying exclusively on coarser pleasures, trying to *consume* happiness in an attempt to sate your restless, needy hungers—too busy pursuing pleasure to notice the joy of *being alive*. In neurological terms, a consumptive lifestyle and a reward-centered nervous system have us addictively chasing the quick pleasure spike of a dopamine hit at the expense of serotonin, the brain chemical associated with genuine well-being, calm, and ease. Joy uplifts the spirit, whereas gratification reinforces the relentless hamster-wheel cycle of desire: pursuit—reward—loss—hunger—repeat.

Look at the world. Ask people what they want and they'll tell you it's happiness. Watch what they actually *do* in the pursuit of that happiness, and you'll see a world full of people (often in the name of *having fun*) desperately trying to buy their way, shop their way, eat and fuck and drink and position their way to feeling OK about themselves. Hollow materialism, loss of spirit, and a savagely degraded environment are the inevitable fallout of our relentless empty pleasure-seeking.

How might your life be transformed, if you could be content? If your heart were nourished by the miracle of having this human experience at all, by the perplexing and profound mystery that *there is a universe*, and you are alive and conscious in it! Mudita is happiness for no good reason. Delighted to be here, because we have no clue as to how long it will last. Appreciative that there is a world (populated by beings!) and that we have this extraordinary apparatus—human body, mind, and spirit—with which to meet the constant everyday miracle of being here.

Cultivating Joy

To open to joy, you have to break your stimulation addiction. You have to cut through your half-defended, half-distracted attention barrier. You have to put down your phone and look up. Put down your habits and *feel in*. Slowing down is one way to do this.

Take a moment now for the following reflection.

Reflection

First inwardly: Sense into the natural feel of being here. Breath and body, and the basic, natural wakefulness of being conscious. Don't take these for granted. Sense them afresh as the miracle they are.

Feel the air on your skin. The contact of your clothes—all those sensitive nerve endings picking up the touch of life.

Now outwardly: Look around you, while staying embodied awareness. Notice the room you're in, or the sky above you. Listen to the sounds of the world unfolding. What a miracle that you can see and hear and feel!

Stay a little while like this. What is the effect on your heart?

Very simply, you can cultivate joy by turning toward sources of joy. Start with whatever is easy for you—it might be in music or art or nature. It might be taking time to lie on the grass and watch the clouds moving across the sky. It might be watching children play or raindrops running down a window.

Attending to everyday detail was more common in those distant pre-smartphone days. It takes a certain discipline now for many of us to put away the endless source of dopamine amusement, information, and entertainment in our pocket, so as to be more available for the sensory life around us. Culturally and individually, we're already experiencing the cost of digital distraction, and I wonder in years to come what we'll make of it all. I love technology—and being on the road more than six months a year, my iPhone is incredibly useful for navigation, buying tickets, staying in touch with my family, and so on. But I increasingly notice the cost on my attention.

With so much to distract us, it is so important to train ourselves in the deep nourishment of nonstimulated joy. This is part of the deep goodness of going on a meditation retreat. We resist the idea of doing without comfort, or talking, or whatever— but when we actually find ourselves in a simple environment, stripped of stimulation and distraction, it is often a profound relief.

As I wrote earlier, with so much time on the road I'm often alone—in restaurants, in parks—watching people in their couples and groups enjoying each other's company. It is easy to generate loneliness and self-pity in some way, but it is also possible to enjoy other people's togetherness and happiness, to watch them with the eyes that rejoice in their friendship, that share in their fun, to be glad for the fact that people find each other, care for each other, love each other.

Joy is one of the *boundless* qualities, meaning there is no limit to our capacity to delight and enjoy. Use any opportunity you get. Dance and celebrate and give thanks for what there is. The blessings of your life are myriad, whatever your circumstances. Your very existence is the confirmation of how much life is loving you, supporting you, blessing you. You are life's fundamental delight in itself.

Upekkha: The Love That Allows

Rather than "equanimity," I prefer to translate the classical Buddhist term *upekkha* as the vastness of the heart—a limitless embrace—an exquisite capacity to make room for anything and everything that arises in experience, to love what is, *whether we like it or not.*

This is a love that feels like infinite space in the heart. Your chest area literally feels unbounded in its welcome. Whatever happens, there is room for it. Everything and anything feels malleable, work-able, digestible, relatable. It may be sweet or sour, pleasurable or painful, and therefore evoke joy or compassion respectively, but whatever it is, it is allowed to be here simply *because it is.* This is a way of paying the deepest respect to life, by allowing what is here to be felt—to arise and pass according to its nature.

Vast like the Ocean

Consciousness is like an ocean—vast and unfathomable, with tides and eddies that form and unform, each experience like a wave—uniquely itself for its brief moment of existence, yet inseparably part of and reflecting the whole ocean. Each wave is important, worthy of care and attention. Yet it is also just a drop, infinitesimal in a vast and essentially placid ocean of being, worthy of attention but never worth fixating upon or contracting around. The free heart is intimate with each wave, embracing without making drama, caring without identifying, honoring each wave while knowing its nature as the whole ocean. In this wide-open love, there is no drama. Each wave expresses the fundamental freedom of experience, and even the deluded thoughts—the needy, greedy, lazy, crazy, merry-go-round of everyday monkey-mind—express this freedom. Waves form, present themselves, and crash onto the shore or sink back into the ocean. There is no disturbance, and the free heart makes room for it all: free of neurotic pulling and pushing; free from the distor-tions of optimism and pessimism, lighthearted when the comfort-able and convenient give way inevitably to the uncomfortable and inconvenient; free from entitlement, demand, and defense; free to love what is, whether we like it or not.

The Bodhisattva of Bodh Gaya

> I took refuge in the understanding that nothing
> can be grasped. Every phenomenon, including
> deluded thoughts, reveals the one true nature
> of buddha and human beings alike.

Out of stillness manifests the capacity to respond
in accord with the inexpressible Dharma and all my
wrestling with distracted thought ends again and again
in the unequivocal embrace of the futility of all search.

—THOMAS JOST, in his last letter, a few days before
his death in retreat in Burma, June 2000

Thomas was a good friend with whom I spent a month each year in the Thai monastery in Bodh Gaya, India, all through the 1990s. He lived in a small hut in the compound of the Burmese Vihara for many months each year in Bodh Gaya, supporting various NGOs and overseeing the Prajna-Vihar ("Abode of Wisdom") interfaith school set up and maintained through the annual month-long retreats at the Thai monastery taught by my teacher Christopher Titmuss. Thomas exemplified the spacious, loving quality of *upekkha*. He gave a gentle, spacious attention to all those he met. I never saw him impatient or harried, uncaring, or insensitive. He walked in long, easy strides that implied he had *plenty of time*, though he managed many responsibilities. He took everything in his stride—and died as simply and openly as he had lived, gently sloughing off this body after getting ill on a long solo retreat in Burma. I am touched by the memory of his presence as I write on the vastness of heart which he expressed so . . . freely.

Nonstick Consciousness

The openness of a free heart means that nothing gets stuck. Whatever arises can be deeply felt, without obsession, without rejection. The usual circus of contraction, fixation, rejection, judgment, and ego-drama looks unnecessary and exhausting, foolish and futile—pathological even.

The sky does not make drama out of weather passing through. The wide-open heart makes similarly effortless and wide-open space for the stuff of everyday mind. There is no contention with experience. No friction. The absence of anxiety about imperfection. You care deeply, but you don't mind. Whatever happens.

In a wide-open heart, vicissitudes don't create agitation. They feel normal and are welcomed. Difficulties are a reminder of the natural order of things, the inevitable gusts of the worldly winds. What a relief, when the uncomfortable is not a surprise or a problem, but rather is just what *is*, right now. When we no longer expect things to "go right," then things "going wrong" no longer makes sense. There are no more problems, because we have ceased looking through that lens, and instead there is just the such-ness of things, just as they are. As Ajahn Sumedho has made his catch-phrase: "Right now, it's like this."

Expand Your Comfort Zone

If my mind is full of self-concern—my wishes, my objections, my beliefs, my justifications and my preferences and my neediness, it is impossible to abide spaciously. If *I/me/mine* gets built up and reinforced until it is completely opaque, then not only can I not see through it, I can't even recognize that there *is* anything beyond it.

An untrained mind fixates on this realm, pulling at what it likes, pushing against what's uncomfortable. The holy trinity of usual fixations are: *I want what I like* (clinging to desire); *I want to be right* (clinging to views and opinions); *I want to feel secure* (clinging to a sense of self).

For most people, these habitual concerns get blindly reinforced (*whatever you feed, that's what grows*), increasing with age and shrinking the comfort zone of what feels manageable or acceptable (that's why old people tend to more attached to their habits and preferences, less politically tolerant, more fixed in their views, and so on).

We treat them almost as a "God-given" right. Pathologically (and highly unrealistically), we expect our interactions with people, places, and situations to please us (*gimme what I want*), to confirm our opinions (*let me be right*), and to reassure us (*I need to feel secure*). The more we expect that, the less open we are, and as a consequence we fall into conflict and polarization.

This shows up most extremely in the particularly American culture of entitlement, where I regularly hear people express the indignation of: *"I'm not comfortable with that."* To which I often internally reply, *"So what?"* Discomfort is part of being human. As the old saying goes, you can try to cover the whole world with leather, or you can get a pair of sandals. To expect that life would arrange itself in conjunction with your pleasure, comfort, and reassurance is to set yourself up for disappointment, offense, and misery.

Reflection

How would it be if you weren't so dependent on getting what you want?

How might it feel, if you didn't need to be right?

Given you are speeding down a one-way street toward certain death, how liberating might it be to embrace the fundamental insecurity of life?

The Worldly Winds

Pleasure and pain, gain and loss, success and failure, praise and blame—these are the currents that blow through all our lives. You may persist in the illusion of a perfect life, but look around you—nobody has ever lived one. Do you really think you might be the first?

You might agree philosophically, but our expectations of pleasure, comfort, and reassurance run deep. When "things go wrong," we tend to blame and panic, instead of seeing that things going wrong *is not wrong—it's perfectly natural!*

My mother used to have the habit, when things went wrong, of exclaiming, "That's typical!" As if it somehow confirmed her view that life had it in for her. Others of us, confronted by the unfortunate or the unpleasant, might exclaim: *"It's not fair!"* Well, no, it isn't. Life's infinite, freely unfolding nature, right now and always, is neither fair nor unfair, it is just . . . *like this*.

Cultivating a Spacious Heart

Any moment, every moment, you have plenty of opportunity to get familiar with the changing vicissitudes of life. Practice attending especially to the momentary flickerings of pleasure and pain, as training wheels for attending to the larger waves that must surely come your way at some point. Acknowledging and integrating the natural flow of the pleasant and unpleasant make for openness and spaciousness—a capacity to be steady in the midst of whatever arises.

Sitting meditation is perhaps the most potent and focused form of cultivating this steadiness. Some people say they meditate whenever they feel like it. That's nice. But what about when you *don't feel like it*? Maybe that's when it could be of greatest benefit, as you learn how to be gracious and spacious with uncomfortable experience— as you learn to be steady in the midst of restlessness, boredom, irritation, and so on. To one who wants a feel-good meditation, these states look like barriers to good practice—in reality these states exactly *are* your practice, when they arise.

Reflection

Notice what happens when a pleasant experience turns sour. What stories do you tell yourself? What inner rhetoric have you developed around disappointment, self-pity, blame, or entitlement?

Spaciousness is a boundless quality of heart. Whatever arises, the very fact that it can be *known and felt*, shows you that there is space for it. Nothing need be excluded from your heart. Upekkha is the heart as wide as the world, a vast spacious love in your chest, a deep, gracious bow to all the various dramas and details that breeze through your life.

8

This Body, This World

Do not ask me where I am going
as I travel in this limitless world
where every step I take is my home

—DOGEN

I began meditating seriously as a teenager, after becoming both fascinated and frustrated by awareness. Fascinated by the mystery of it, frustrated by the seeming impossibility of apprehending my own mind and its nature.

At high school, I had a fifteen-minute walk home along a busy main road from the bus stop. Cars sped past me and, with no sidewalk, their dangerous proximity became a daily contemplation on life, death, and the nature of consciousness: What would happen, I kept asking myself, if I stepped into the path of a car? I felt so alive—so conscious, so mysteriously and unmistakably *here*. And yet a single step sideways would surely be fatal. What would happen? Where would this consciousness go? Beyond physical extinction, "death" seemed vague as a concept, yet somehow compelling and mysterious. What would happen? *What would end?*

Of course, nobody could tell me. You'd have to ask the dead themselves (and they, of course, are not talking). Parents, teachers, and friends encouraged me gently (and tediously) to apply for university ("business studies, perhaps?") and, er, to stop walking down that road, both literally and figuratively. They assumed I had some worrying death wish, but actually I'd never felt so alive, awake, and conscious.

Those daily downhill "meditations" formed themselves into compelling questions about the nature of self and world, subjectivity and reality:

- What is consciousness?
- What is the difference between consciousness and mind?
- Who am I?
- Am I my mind, or am I what is conscious of my mind, or am I a product of having a conscious mind?

And equally:

- What is the world?
- Is what I see real and "out there," or is my sense of the world merely a product of my own interpretations? A kind of dream?
- Is "my world" the same as or different from others' worlds?

These questions began to supersede all concerns and interests. I just about completed high school, worked as a milkman for a few months to save some money, and in late 1988 left for Cairo with a one-way ticket and precisely no luggage. I'm not quite sure why Egypt (I think *Raiders of the Lost Ark* had something to do with it—I found something of a fantasy alter ego in Indiana Jones), but I did know I wanted to get out. Out of Europe, out of the way, out of the oppression of the comfortable and the familiar. I wanted to explore myself, by way of exploring the world.

Amid all the important, formative experiences of those first months on the road, two experiences in particular stand out:

The first was at Mount Sinai, where the Bible has Moses receiving the ten commandments.* I spent one cold, beautiful night under an intensely starry sky on the summit, and walking down the following morning, I was already struck by my infinitesimal smallness and insignificance. In a self-reinforcing loop (*me, me, me!*), my mind's familiar stories usually created the boundaries by which I defined myself, yet these limitations seemed coarse and clumsy in the vast, edgeless desert. The empty blue sky was infinitely open, reality was made timeless in the ancient landscape and biblical history.

Someone I was walking down with took a letter from his bag. He read aloud as his mother complained of a broken washing machine, a family argument, a delay to a wedding. Those things needed attention in her world, yet against the desert backdrop of an infinitely mysterious universe they seemed suddenly nonsensical—grotesque evidence of how we lock ourselves in a prison of our own making, small-minded and self-absorbed, while life's fundamental freedom unfolds all around us—within us—*as us*. Seeing this clearly, the fire of some intimacy always longed for suddenly blazed up, turning my usual self-referencing to ash, blown away into the desert air. I was gone for a brief, timeless moment, lost to myself yet found in each grain of sand, each gust of wind. Undone, deconstructed, yet exhilarated. Free from myself. Inside out. Gone.

As I continued the walk downhill, while a more usual self-consciousness slowly reconstructed itself, a clear vow nevertheless crystallized in my heart: Washing machines wouldn't claim me, personal concerns wouldn't control me. Desert and stars, limitless space, wide-open mystery would be my only home.

I traveled for eight months through Egypt, Jordan, Israel, Turkey. I often met people who had been to India, their descriptions conjuring up some fantasyland of mystery and mysticism. One day, a guy in a Bedouin camp in Dahab said to me, "If you go to India, man, it'll turn you inside out." And that was the second pivotal moment.

---

* Was this the first download from the cloud, onto a tablet?

Inside out! That is how I had felt coming down from Mount Sinai. That's how I wanted to live, with my heart exposed to life like the Hindu monkey god Hanuman, tearing open his chest to reveal Rama and Sita inside.

I knew nothing of India except vague impressions of turbans and temples (*Indiana Jones* again?), which were now replaced with fantasies of fakirs and gurus, Himalayan hermits, and cave-dwelling ascetics—people dedicated to contemplation, to knowing God, *to understanding consciousness!*

I went back to the UK for three months and worked in a life insurance office (as distinctly un-free a feeling as I had ever known), and left for Delhi in December 1989. The Berlin Wall had just come down. Freedom was in the air. I had been reading about Buddhism and meditation (and constructing wildly inaccurate ideas about both). After a month or so of distracting myself in Goa with dancing, flirting, and LSD (separately and together), I went up to Dharamsala in the Himalayan foothills to get serious.

And then I finally sat down with myself. The first time I ever crossed my legs in a meditation hall, the first minutes of the first teachings I ever heard, the first bow before a golden buddha image in a gentle haze of incense and offerings, I knew I had found my path. Like water in the desert, here was a whole stream of teachings and practices for exploring, training, and understanding one's own mind—for penetrating the mysteries of reality. Here were tools and teachings for the endless adventure of confronting my own inner lack of freedom, and transforming it.

WHAT IS REAL?

We look at a universe supposedly "out there"—a world populated with people, other beings, and countless objects, from the cup of tea in front of me now to infinitely distant planets and galaxies. We meet this world at our "sense doors"—seeing, hearing, smelling, tasting, and touching whatever is in our reach. This is all so normal and ordinary that it seems incontrovertible: *I am a self, moving around in a world, experiencing it with my senses, and telling myself about it with my mind.*

But is that the *truth*—or just perceptual habit? A convenient reduction to manage infinite sensory data? Given the vast, unfathomable nature of life, no wonder our mental apparatus would divide experience into manageable chunks: Self and world—time, space, and objects.

Self and *world* are the most fundamental reference points for our sense of reality. There is nothing more primary. Right now, as you read these words: The sense of self is immediate and obvious—*I am.* You can feel your body. You instinctively recognize the awakeness of your mind. Sensory perception, memory, imagination, and thought fill in all the gaps and construct a coherent sense both of an inner self and an outer world. Amazing!

Every moment's ordinary experience is an *extra*-ordinarily sophisticated interrelationship of experience, perception, and interpretation, which the meditative traditions ask us to question. Rather than going round and round in speculation (which does nothing to alter the sense of self and world), we can contemplate these two poles of reality directly. When we do, we find they can appear in all kinds of different forms. There are (at least) four main modes of perception—in other words, four ways that the sense of self and the sense of world can appear, disappear, and interact with each other. I'll call them, respectively, *self-centered, self-absorbed, self-less,* and *gone beyond.*

Self-centered: This is the mode of everyday perception—there's a clear sense of both inner subject (self) and outer object (world): *I'm sitting here, seeing and interacting with the world around me.* This is everyday reality mode—the relationship you have with being here now, reading these words. The subjective position of self as observer seems obvious and feels real (check it out now in your own experience), as does the objective world around me (look around you to make sure!). We reinforce this perception in our thought, speech, and worldview, all of which adds to its seeming obviousness, so much so that it seems ontologically true: *There is a self and a world* that somehow both exist and interact. This mode is so primary it becomes concretized as *the true version* of reality. The existence of self and world are unquestioned.

Self-absorbed: Here there is *all self, no world.* We all know this experience: You might get completely absorbed in replaying yesterday's argument with your friend or totally caught up in doubt or self-judgment. You might get utterly seduced by some fantasy or pulled into worrying about a future situation, so much so that the world actually disappears. You no longer hear sounds, you don't notice time passing—you are utterly caught up in self-preoccupation. This feeling of being absorbed in (or *lost* in) your thoughts can be both deeply unpleasant and anxiety provoking (obsessive-compulsive thoughts, paranoia). It can also be pleasant (daydream, fantasy), but even when one is lost in some delicious reverie, the process itself soon starts to feel unsatisfactory. One of the most common reasons for starting to meditate is because "I am too much in my head."

This happens particularly intensely for teenagers. Their sense of self is still nebulous, and they spend much of their time and energy trying to figure out who they are, or *what this self is?* Questioning one's self-identity is a normal, important, and psychologically stage-appropriate concern for teenagers, as they wobble across the threshold from childhood to adulthood. But growing up in a culture that is predominantly and increasingly *materialistic* (there is nothing beyond what can be seen and touched) and *atheistic* (there is no meaning or existence beyond one's own life) exacerbates self-absorption. And if *it's all about me,* then that places a terrible pressure on the *me* in question. More and more teenagers find this pressure intolerable, contributing to growing levels of self-harm among adolescents (22 percent of fourteen-year-old girls, according to one recent UK study). Young people hurt themselves physically to divert their attention from their emotional pain. Caught up in their inner drama, they inflict physical pain as a way to *return to the sensory world* that their self-absorption has taken them away from. It's distressing to see how the individualism, secularism, and consumerism of current culture encourage pathological-strength self-absorption, whatever our age.

Self-less—all world, no self: Have you ever lost yourself in a sunset or a piece of music? Danced until you disappeared? Maybe you have sat some time, absorbed in a mountain view like the Chinese poet Li Bai, from the first century CE:

> We sit here together
> The mountain and I, 'til only
> The mountain remains

There are many ways to disappear. Various trance states can induce this feeling, and meditation practice can also produce a perceptual shift wherein the duality of self and world dissolves. Sometimes people feel frightened and disoriented by this kind of self-disappearance. If that happens, the fear makes you self-conscious and quickly draws you back into a more familiar sense of self and world. More often though, people experience this self-forgetting as a great relief—a blessed respite from the relentless blah-blah of their inner discourse. When self disappears, the world is peaceful and still and, somehow, inherently good and beautiful. Reality appears to hold all of existence both effortlessly and tenderly, as in a gentle, maternal embrace. The world is good, and the self is at peace.

Gone beyond: No self, no world. This is the least common state, and the hardest to speak about, but it is a reality of the nature of consciousness. The most accessible way to speak about it is with deep sleep. What happens to the self when your conscious experience is gone? What happens to the world? You can speculate *philosophically* about their continued existence, but *experientially*, both vanish. When you are deeply asleep, you are gone. The world is gone. Nothing is left. And then, amazingly, both reference points reconfigure themselves again the next morning, reinforcing the sense of continuity, as if both had somehow been there all the time.

Meditation opens up other ways of disappearing both self and world. In the condition of *nirodha*, or cessation, there is a perceptual stopping. Self and world are gone. For a timeless moment, no reference points of reality impinge on consciousness. One cannot even say that there is consciousness. Interestingly, the meditative (non) experience of *nirodha* is exquisitely refreshing, as if your nervous system has been utterly refreshed and reset.

TRANSFIGURING SELF AND WORLD

Despite our assumptions of self and world as stable entities, we've just seen that each can appear and disappear in our experience. Given this malleability, we could ask then: *What is a true experience of self and world?* but then we trap ourselves in a philosophical cul-de-sac. I would rather ask, what are *useful* ways of experiencing these two reference points for reality? How can you dissolve the sense of difference, defensiveness, and division between the two? How can you experience self and world in ways that cultivate harmony, openness, and love?

We have been designing our experience (or having it designed for us) for a very long time. Have you visited any of the great European cathedrals, like Canterbury or Notre Dame? Enter in and there is an immediate transfiguration of self and world—the former shrinks, its smallness and insignificance reinforced. The latter assumes vast, powerful, divine dimensions. If you have been awed by stepping into a vast religious space like this, then imagine how it would have been for a country-dwelling peasant, a thousand years ago. Familiar with rough stone walls and a thatched roof, those vast vaulted ceilings would have felt like proof incarnate of God's existence. (It is also a power-play. Make the world of the cathedral feel huge and powerful, and you make the poor sinner entering in feel small and weak. The same thing plays out with building design nowadays, though our secular cathedrals are the glass and steel corporate towers where we worship consumerism and pray with money.)

We can curate our experience of self and world in more intimate, human-scale ways. Some years ago, I spent a week in London, traveling at commuter times. The morning subway rides felt dreary and oppressive. My sense of self felt burdened by the heavy silence, my sense of the world took on a gray, monotonous feel. Seeing how unhelpful this was, I looked for a way to *redesign* my experience of self and world in that particular situation—to meet experience in a way that would produce a more harmonious sense, a more intimate sense, a more *helpful* sense of self and world.

I began to listen to choral music on those journeys—mostly Arvo Pärt and Hildegard von Bingen—and it totally transformed the experience. The ethereal tones created a kind of energetic cathedral right there in what had previously been a dirty train. Against the backdrop of exquisite vocal harmonies, each being looked angelic. The doors would slide open at a station, and *whoosh!*—angels would glide out of the train while others glided in. Everything seemed effortless—divinely orchestrated. The world was transfigured—a realm of purity and beauty populated by beings of grace. Self was transformed into the bright pure witness of this great angelic play, abiding as peace and clear awareness.

Which version of that Tube journey was the "true" one? Of course it doesn't matter. The first way of experiencing it cultivated feelings of frustration and depression. The second way cultivated love for my fellow beings, a sense of wonder about the world and of intimacy with all things.

Consider the various situations of your own life, particularly those in which you get caught in a difficult or unhelpful sense of your self or the world. How do your habits feed those familiar views, and how might you meet them differently? More freely?

THE WHOLE WORLD IS RIGHT HERE

All experience is right here. Everything we call *self* (physical, mental, and emotional experience) and everything we call *world* (the seen, the heard, the felt, and the imagined), it is all happening *here*, in this body of experience. And *here* is infinite. Either inwardly or outwardly, can you find the edges of *right here?* (Not in your ideas—in

your actual experience.) We create measures of distance in milli-
meters or kilometers and categories called "inner" and "outer," but
where does all experience present itself? Where has everything you
have ever seen, heard, and imagined ever taken place? Right here.
Here in awareness—here in this field of conscious experience that we
call mind. Here in this body. *Right here* is where all of life shows up.

You have never had a single experience that was anywhere other
than right here. You *cannot* experience anything other than this. You
may object, pointing to all kinds of externalities: "Well, right now,
I'm looking at this book in my hands, and at the room around me.
They are not my body, they are *out there*!" But where is *looking* happening? Be truly intimate for a moment with the seeing and the seen.
Inner and outer, book and eye, self and world are all right here. There
is no escape from this. You have never been elsewhere. There is no
other place. *Wherever you go, there you are*, as the title of Jon Kabat-
Zinn's classic book succinctly tells us. Everything has greeted you in
the profound *here-ness* of your life.

Reflection

Pause for a moment, right here. Listen to the sounds around you—
whether birdsong or traffic, people on the street or elsewhere in your
building, the hum of the refrigerator, the quiet rhythm of your breathing.
Listen closely. Let yourself feel the right-here-ness, the immediacy of the
sounds. Take a few moments to really listen, both outwardly and inwardly.

Listen like this, and you probably notice how quickly and easily thinking imposes itself. We describe and analyze like a sports
commentator watching the game of our own lives. "Oh, there are
the neighbor's footsteps on the floor above me, I can hear her high-
heeled shoes." We question, trying to reduce the unknown to the
familiar: "What is that sound? Where do I recognize it from?" We
create layers of conditioned images, ideas, and reactions, reinforcing

our familiar world. Yet this default mode—making sense of experience through a constant stream of thinking about ourselves, each other, and the world—is only a way station along the path of a still developing human consciousness, albeit one where most people move in and settle down, mistaking it for the destination.

The Buddha is often quoted as saying, "If you could understand a single flower, you would understand the whole Universe." Actually it's a very common misquote, perhaps related to the Zen story about the Buddha holding up a single flower. This line derives from Tennyson, in his poem "Flower in the Crannied Wall," but the point stands. Open up anything, and everything opens up. Penetrate any experience, and we start to see the nature of all experience. Self and world and the whole universe with all their mysteries are available right here in your current experience.

Your Infinite Body

> I searched for God and found only myself.
> I searched for myself and found only God.
>
> —Sufi proverb

When I was first getting interested in consciousness as a teenager, I wrote a poem about the benefits of intentionally doing nothing, partly inspired by reading Camus's *The Plague*, wherein one of the characters makes a whole art form of doing nothing, so as to be closer to his experience. Here is part of what I wrote:

> So you spend all day on a hard wooden chair
> In a nameless waiting room
> Or you sit outside on your balcony
> The whole of an afternoon
> And the rats they leave your sinking ship
> Your friends all pass you by
> But still you watch and wait to see
> What sees behind the *I*

What infinite mysteries *lie behind the I?* Everyday mind reinforces the familiar sense of self and world, subject and object, inner and outer, but putting the familiar aside and listening with meditative attention, I cannot find where a sound ends and the hearing of it begins—where the outer world stops and the inner starts. The division between *me* and *not-me* begins to soften. Sounds are right here, in the intimacy of awareness.

Sight is the most dominant sense in reinforcing the familiar though various optical illusions show us the arbitrariness of visual perception—a vase can also be two faces, the dress that some are sure is blue and black, others clearly see as white and gold. Perception is uncertain, ambiguous, conditioned.

Look around you now, at this page and at your surroundings. See what you notice. Habitually, attention focuses on the recognizable, the *objectifiable*. Right now, my gaze falls on the glow of the screen I am writing on, the cup of green tea faintly steaming on my desk— my fingers, now resting while I think, now typing these words—the trees outside my window in their varied forms and shades of green, and above them a few small clouds floating in the blue expanse of sky.

The nearer and more tangible the object, the more it compels the attention. The tea cup is very directly relatable. I can touch it, taste it, move it around. Take charge of it. In this way it easily reinforces my sense of a world I can affect, one which I can—*and want to*— control. The more distant objects, and those which don't affect me so directly, make much less impact on my senses. It would be easy to ignore both trees and sky, unless for example there is a sudden storm and they start to impact me more.

Attending to less compelling objects, however, can open up a more intimate knowing. Look contemplatively and you notice the *space between* objects. Whatever you see, however much you fixate upon various objects, the vast majority of all your visual field is non-object: empty, open space. You might see that you can only identify objects *because of* the space around them.

Space is infinite. Looking outward, we call this infinity "the world," or "outer space." Going inward, we call it "consciousness," or "inner space." Whether we go out or in, though, we find the same spacious nature, infinite and ungraspable.

Open space is a valuable focus for awareness. Gaze awhile on *no-thing*. Look into the spaces between, and you begin to feel the *quality* of spaciousness itself, which is an inherent characteristic of both consciousness and the world of objects. Feel the nonstimulation, the nondemand of no-object. Empty space has always been important in the contemplative traditions. Desert expanses, mountain vistas, the open sky. To meditate on infinite space is to gaze beyond the limitations of everyday mind, to rest in ungraspable infinity.

Gaze into a night sky and you'll see the vast reach of the universe of "outer infinity," which we call space. Gaze into your mind, and you'll see the vast reach of "inner infinity" that we call consciousness. It's infinity either way. No edge or center. No inner or outer. Just this!

GATEWAYS TO INFINITY

Buddha brilliantly broke down the different processes which make up our human experience. The five *khandas*—a Pali word that means "composites"—are a way of both understanding experience and, more significantly, *sensing into* its fluidity, its *non-thing-ness*. Everything you have ever or could ever experience is included and described by these five interweaving processes. These five composites of reality apply equally to what we call inner and outer. Their contemplation guides a transition from a world of separated objects, known by a conscious subject, to an infinite realm of presence and process, where everything interpenetrates. Sense into these elements in your own experience, as we go through them:

Physical/sensory experience: All that is seen, heard, felt, smelled, imagined, and conceived. For instance, this book, being seen right now.

Affective experience: The pleasure or pain response, the pleasant, unpleasant, or neutral impact of all that enters consciousness. For instance, the liking or not liking (or being indifferent to) what you're reading right now.

Perceptive experience: Eyes meeting sights, ears meeting sounds. Memory and cognition label and define the fluidity of experience and tell us what is happening. For instance, recognizing this as a book, being able to make sense of the printed signs, render them into words, and make meaning out of them, right now.

Mental/emotional experience: Attitudes, moods, emotions. The way we interpret and add layers to experience, giving it personal importance and meaning. For instance, what you think about this book, its author, or the teachings in it, and whatever personal investment you have in what you have read and reflected on, your agreement or disagreement with the ideas you are taking in, right now.

Consciousness: The immediacy of being conscious—the knowing that arises as the cognition of each moment, of all experience. Consciousness has no location, except *here.* We can't locate it (even though we are often convinced it lives in our heads). It is unfindable, yet incredibly *available,* underpinning every aspect of experience: This *khanda* is apparent in the fact that you can recognize any experience at all, right now, it includes the basic knowing of being here, of holding this book, of reading these words.

The constant is experience. All that we call self and world and all of reality appear as physical, affective, perceptual, mental-emotional, conscious *experience.* Make this your home—the infinite realm of experience—the always available open door to deepening, opening, liberating whatever's happening here. Outer and inner dissolve into one another in direct experience. The gap between self and world resolves in the infinite embrace of experience.

Your body is the universe.

9

This Dying Body

Someone gave me a cartoon strip once, which I hung for a while in the Moulin office. The first drawing shows a child playing, with the caption: *Too young to meditate*. The next features young lovers, and underneath: *Too much in love to meditate*. It continues with the image of someone at their computer, who's *Too busy to meditate*, and continues in a similar vein through various life situations and stages. The last image is of a gravestone, and the caption? *Too late to meditate*...

RELAX! YOU'LL SOON BE GONE

As the old saying goes, "the cemeteries are full of once indispensable people." We know absolutely that we are hurtling at an unknown speed down a one-way street toward our certain demise, yet we avoid the subject and the reality of death. Reflecting on our mortal nature is considered morbid or depressive, whereas exactly the opposite can be true. If you really see clearly how fragile and precious this life is, you value each moment, you take nothing for granted, you live in the light of that seeing, marveling at each day, and at the miracle that you are here for it.

In a monastery where I stayed in Thailand, a rough handmade sign hung from a tree which read: *Relax! In a hundred years, all new people.*

Perhaps counterintuitively, contemplating death can indeed be relaxing and relieving. Taking our lives so seriously, we generate all kinds of tension and pressure that we are so used to that they seem normal, yet which turn out to be both unhelpful and unnecessary. When you contemplate that you'll soon be gone—any day, or any decade now—the first layer of that reflection is often one of fear—of the unknown—of nonexistence. Yet as you get familiar with it, the clear acknowledgment of your mortality can become your friend.

Once, while walking through the graveyard of an old English church with my teacher, we looked together at the mass of tombstones. Some were ancient, fallen, and broken. Some were partly covered in lichen and ivy, while others were well kept and tended, and some still had the fresh mound of earth where they had been only recently filled, flowers just beginning to wilt at the base. Christopher pointed to all the birth dates and death dates inscribed on the various headstones and to the little line between the two dates. "That line," he said. "That's what all of our human lives get reduced to."

Within a generation or two, that's all that's left. All the drama and detail, the love and loss, joy and sorrow—reduced to that short dash between birth and death.

MARANASATI

You'll find nobody who can tell you much about death. I like Ram Dass's hunch, whom I once heard say that his best sense is, it's like taking off a tight shoe at the end of a long day. A sweet relief to expand beyond the narrow confines of these three cubic feet of bone and blood and meat. While we cannot really anticipate death, there are several contemplations that are really helpful in facing wide awake into the open mouth of King Yama, the Buddhist representation of death (a bit like the Grim Reaper).

Aging: Yes, it's happening to all of us, despite a multibillion-dollar industry helping people to be in great denial of the fact, with all kinds of antiaging products. Antiaging! Really? Can you stop a day from passing? We fetishize youth to the exact degree that we refuse to face the truth of our changing, aging, decaying, bodily reality. Students often tell me of their anxiety or distress about the sagging, graying, stiffening, weakening truth of bodily change—the unstoppable atrophying of all that was once firm and supple and smooth. This gets magnified by looking backward nostalgically to *how I was* (though the chances are you didn't really appreciate that at the time—like Oscar Wilde reminds us, "Youth is wasted on the young.") and by looking forward fearfully to *how I'll be*. Dharma practice asks you to look clearly into the present, in which you might see that *this moment is the most youthful you'll ever be. This is the youngest moment of the rest of your life. Enjoy it.*

Attend to the truth of aging. Look closely at your changing face, your hair, your skin (you may need spectacles!). Let yourself feel into the fear or ambivalence or disgust that might arise in some moments. Let yourself also rest into the richness of your accumulated life experience. You might like the idea of getting your twenty-year-old body back, but would you really want the twenty-year-old mind that went with it? There is goodness to the life you've lived your way into. Not knowing how much longer it will last, can you let yourself feel and trust that goodness?

I was talking with an elderly student recently, who after a stroke is unable to look after himself physically. Still bright-minded, he struggled to accept being washed, fed, wiped, and changed. Like Shakespeare's seven ages of a human life, we sometimes finish as we began, helpless like a baby, dependent on others for our most basic needs. This can be either torturous or touching, depending on how you face it. "Hang on," I told him, "and this will feel humiliating. Let go, and you can be humbled by all the care and love and attention you're being given."

This is the difference between aging resentfully or freely; humiliatingly or humbly. Aging is happening day by day, skin creams, hair dye, and Botox notwithstanding. To age well is not measured in wrinkles but in living graciously inside your body as it is, moment by changing moment. Day by ever-closer-to-your-last day.

Attending to endings is a powerful practice—the last mouthful of a meal, the close of each day, the coming to rest of every out-breath. There are myriad opportunities to contemplate the natural arising-expressing-passing cycle of all phenomena. If you make this part of your practice, it usually unfolds in two parts. First, it's all death. You see and feel the poignancy if this everywhere. Every flower wilts. Each moment disappears. Every life ends. You might very keenly feel a sense of loss and tragedy—every single expression of life constantly slipping away and collapsing. This can at first seem depressing or nihilistic, but when you stay with that heart-wrenching loss, then right here the second part comes into focus: Life is ever new. Self-generating, fertile, dynamic, ceaseless, irrepressibly creative—everything is constantly reinventing itself. You can feel life's effulgence in every cell of your body and in all things that come to consciousness. You find out in fact that *you are* life's effulgence. All *things* will pass—this day, this body, this planet, this solar system. But *life* is undaunted, unthwarted, unstoppable—the infinite container of all comings and goings. Life *itself* is the fundamental ground of your being. *You* are on your way out, but the life that animates you is utterly irrepressible. Feel it. Trust it. Live it. Or rather, let it live you.

HEAVENLY MESSENGERS

In the life story of the Buddha, having grown up in a cosseted atmosphere of wealth and privilege, he is existentially startled by encountering an old person, a sick person, and a dead person and, realizing that he too shares this inevitable fate, feels compelled to explore his life more deeply.

The Buddhist tradition calls these reminders the *heavenly messengers*, because they call us to a deeper way of life. Aging, sickness, and death will come to us all, but we don't have to be pulled along by a life lived unconsciously and reactively. After seeing the first three people, Buddha then encounters a fourth heavenly messenger, a wandering yogi meditator, challenging him to undertake his own transformational journey.

Someone asked me about going off to the Himalayas to practice, but was anxious about discomfort and inconvenience. I told them, if that's what really called you, go for it. And if you're overly concerned about discomfort and inconvenience, don't go. You can torture yourself worrying about things going wrong, or you can take clear steps in whatever direction seems genuinely important to you. And if you do that, what's the worst that could happen, really? You'd die with your heart directed toward its deepest desire. That might sound dramatic, but most fundamentally, death is not a tragedy. It's natural, and it's coming for you anyway, sooner or later. You can try to keep yourself safe and comfortable—and be run over by a bus tomorrow. Or you can do what lights up your heart and calls you with what seems the deepest and truest and most full of meaning, and see what happens along the way.

In other words, wake up or die trying. It's what we're all doing anyway. We are all of us corpses-in-waiting. You can live in denial of your impending death or be wide awake to it. Death is not a tragedy—it is the natural fate of all living things. And there is no guaranteed amount of time. It is just as natural to die by accident, injury or illness as it is to die of a long life. The tragedy is in the pain of those left behind, when we try to make sense of our loss through the haunting feeling of our own unresolved fear of death and our discomfort with the fact that we have no way of controlling our destiny as we edge imperceptibly but absolutely certainly toward our own final demise.

Cultivating some ease and wakefulness of mortality is also helpful for others—when a family member or other loved one is close to death, for example, it is an immense support to the person slipping away if you can be a fearless, gentle, and reassuring presence—especially if others are being "psychically noisy" with their incapacity to welcome and digest their own fear and grief. To hold someone's hand as they struggle with their last breaths—to stroke their hair as they lie unconscious—to speak gentle words of appreciation for who they have been, even if you are unsure if they can hear them—to tell someone how much they are loved, or let them know they are free to go—these wise and caring gestures can be of immeasurable support.

I had a dear friend who died of cancer, aged thirty-two, when her two children were four and two years old. I arrived at the house hours after her death and, together with her husband, sat and sang and spoke to her, meditated and chanted, and generally "hung out" with whatever was going on in the room in which her corpse lay, for the next three days. We didn't try to rationalize what state she might have been in. Her presence seemed palpable in the room the first day, changing and diminishing over the next seventy-two hours. We just stayed present with whatever came. Our memories of her—our love for her—the grief and sadness that passed through from time to time, in our own hearts and those who passed by to pay their respects. We spoke of her wonderful qualities. Her girlfriends came and bathed and dressed her, painted her nails and brushed her hair. We cared for her in her passing, and in doing so cared for our shared sadness and loss. We met death directly, as she had herself. In her final weeks, she had woven her own coffin from willow, and designed her own funeral, which I was to lead. There was great sadness and poignancy in her passing, yet also a profound knowing that this is what happens. None of us are getting out of here alive.

Living Fully, Dying Freely

If we feel tension or unease in contemplating our mortality, it is born of disquiet about how our life is unlived and unloved—the aspects that are unfulfilled and unresolved—the ways we have gone unconscious, hidden from ourselves, not dared to come forth with who we have secretly longed to be. On the other hand, if you know you have inhabited life fully, death feels like a natural completion of the circle. The more fully and openly you're meeting life, the freer you are to bow out graciously.

I remember being deeply inspired when I heard of Mahatma Gandhi's response to being shot and left for dead with four bullets at point-blank range. He fell instantly to the ground, his hand to his chest, saying "*Hari Ram, Hari Ram.*" That means, "Praise God, Praise God." It's a form of mantra used to turn one's attention away from self-preoccupations, toward a surrender to, and merging with, the Divine.

That's the feeling I have. In moments of danger when death has felt close, there is a brief jolt of alarm or panic as the natural survival mechanism kicks in, adrenalizing the nervous system briefly. But as soon as the contraction and stress in it are recognized, a certain relaxation and peace descend on me—a kind of surrender. If this is my moment to go, the sense is, then let me go freely, as I have tried to live. I trust that surrender deeply, though I don't fool myself into believing that *is* how I'll die. It's impossible to know. I'll only find out when the moment comes, and then I won't be able to report back. At intense moments though, I have seen many times in myself and in others how core habits come to the fore. If you invest mostly in drama and neurosis, avoidance and agitation, desires and distractions, then that's what will come forth—when the going gets tough, the habits get stronger. If, on the other hand, your habit is to cultivate spaciousness and wisdom, patience and surrender, kindness and ease, then that is what will come forth. *Whatever you feed, that's what grows.*

Take care of your precious human life—you don't know how long it will last. These pages contain teachings and practices for knowing an *unimaginable* capacity to live fully and die freely. As my teacher Christopher Titmuss used to say to me: "Teachings and practices, practices and teachings; liberation is unstoppable."

Take note before it is too late.

Afterword

A Free Body

Most essentially, we all want to be free; to know and taste an authentic freeness of being. With only the vaguest sense of what it might be, we search in vain, hoping to find it in our connection with people, places, and experiences. Our freedom of being won't be found in any particular experience, but we keep on hoping. Some of us get seduced by the momentary thrill of exhilaration, which has a passing whiff of freeness. It might be through sport, or sex, or anything else that gives us a good dopamine hit. Others are less motivated by the gratification of pursuing pleasure and are rather trying to get free of themselves by outrunning our pain, hurt, and confusion.

Yet all the while we are pulling for pleasure or pushing against pain, there is inevitably some pressure, some conflict and friction. What *is*, isn't enough. What's *now* won't do. I have to get somewhere, get something, become someone, prove something. And then . . . maybe. Hopefully. Once I've gotten, made, created, resolved, controlled, attained, and eliminated enough, maybe then I'll feel free, I'll be at peace, I'll be OK.

And thus we run on the hamster wheel of samsara. Have you ever watched a hamster on its wheel? It looks very earnest. Convinced it is really getting somewhere. Humans too. We pursue pleasure and run from pain, we demand and defend and distract ourselves in depressingly familiar circles, and the heart's longing for freedom goes tragically unmet, unacknowledged, unfulfilled.

So What Would It Be to Live Freely?

Free from our habits and conditioning.

Free from the blinders and prejudices that color how we see others.

Free from our fears and neuroses, our secret shames, our jealousies, comparisons, and judgments.

Free to meet life as it is in each moment.

Free to love ourselves, while still holding ourselves accountable.

Free to love others, even when we don't like them.

Free to love life, so much so as to lose ourselves in its embrace.

Free to open our hearts to the world with its boundless beauty and tragedy.

Free to die with a heart wide open, whenever that time comes.

That is the path you are invited to walk. It is a path that has been sought, discovered, and explored by people all through history—by those who wouldn't and couldn't settle for convention and conformity, by those who have dared first to dream, and then to commit, to find and follow a path that leads us from a narrow vision of self and world, pleasure and pain, gain and loss, into unimaginable vistas and new realms of freeness.

It is a path in my case, that has several inroads—first and most formally my thirty years exploring in various spiritual practices and traditions, mostly Buddhist but with very porous boundaries—second being a partner and parent for the last twenty-five years, practicing in the up-close and intensive laboratory of family life. And most essentially, of course, the path of being human, with its mystery, wonder, and possibility, daring to listen and respond to the longing of the heart for genuine fulfillment.

SOME AUTOBIOGRAPHICAL UN-FREENESS

I always wanted to be free.

I couldn't always articulate it as that, but even as a child, the pulls and pushes on my psyche were all tugging at that most essential of longings—to know a free moment, an unconstrained experience, a liberated life.

First of all, it was swimming. Childhood asthma made me clumsy and breathless when exerting myself on land. While friends played football or cricket in the street where we lived, I stayed indoors and read fiction, which itself felt like an entryway to a freer world of imagination. And then I went to my local swimming pool and discovered a whole new world—a realm of freeness, the feeling of ease and grace of my body in water—how a flick of the feet could propel me along, the way I could make the noise of the world vanish by holding my breath and disappearing under the surface. Those moments in the water were like a sudden swing toward the true north of freedom, and looking back now I can see how that first taste was already setting course for the compass of my heart.

Theater was the next big passion of my youth. All through teenage life both school and home felt mostly oppressive. Education seemed to bypass the passions and inspirations of the heart in favor of dates, details, diagrams, and dullness. Home was loving, stable, and safe, but whereas my parents were conservative and conformist, I yearned for different, other, foreign, and exotic (ciphers, all, for freeness). Theater gave me a chance to explore inner life, to play and experiment with ways of being—the freedom to take on a role, to become another, most essentially to find a freedom from myself. I was hugely fortunate to have several helpful mentors, at school and at the weekend theater group I attended. In the midst of my middle-class, middle-England, middling life, here were people suddenly with breadth of vision, with artistic sensibilities, with strong political convictions, with expansive, inclusive, and evocative views on life and art and possibility.

The freedom of the drama studio sustained and nourished me until about seventeen years old, when things started to fall apart. Attending a residential drama summer school, a group of us were found partying and drinking and in each other's beds. With us being minors, the staff and particularly the director we were working with of course had a duty of care toward us. Various threats to our future prospects were made to get us to tow the line, and suddenly, theater too felt oppressive, conformist, and unfree. That which had opened up so much for me was suddenly a closed realm. I walked offstage in the middle of a scene the following day and never went back.

For the following couple of years, the weight of being human, of being young and full of possibility yet obviously and painfully unfree, pushed down on me. I was hungry for depth and meaning, and I didn't know where on earth to look. The compass was swinging wildly, and I couldn't see north.

I described in chapter 8 how this adolescent angst ignited in me a deep, unquiet questioning, and the restlessness that propelled me to travel and to discover Buddha's teachings and path of practice. And ever since, I've been walking that path as sincerely as I can. Buddhist teachings most clearly show the way, and teachers, mentors, friends, and family have all helped to clear the track, even when (maybe most especially when) I have thought they were obstructing it.

The Buddhist origins of this book will be very clear to anyone familiar with the tradition. Most fundamentally though, I cannot say it is a Buddhist path I have walked, nor is that what I offer here. Traditions and teachings, Buddhist or otherwise, often clamor to claim the path as their own. They will tell us they have the surest path or the most authentic path. The purest or the oldest or the most mystical path, the one that climbs the mountain the quickest or that leads on the furthest.

Bullshit. Real freedom by its nature is too free to be bound by a particular tradition or teacher or belief system. Freeness is too free to be reduced to a particular approach. If it is true that there is only one way, it is not this way or that. The only real way is the one you make your own.

In walking you through these pages, it has not been my intention to impart some truth or to stake some claim to a particular way. It is to arrive again and again in the land of your direct experience, to explore the terrain of your heart and mind, your sense of self and world, of experience and freedom. I'm happy to share what I have found, and continue to find, and hopefully to have supported you in taking your own steps.

The central aim has been to invite you into the freedom of being that is your human fulfillment. These ink-covered pages are offered in the service of you living more fully, more fluidly, more freely.

May it be so.

Index

About the Author

Martin Aylward traveled to India at age nineteen to explore meditation. He spent most of the next five years in monasteries, ashrams, and meditation centers in India and Thailand, including two years in a hermitage in the Himalayas with one of his teachers. As well as having the good fortune to learn from and practice with many different teachers, both Asian and Western, Martin has spent much time in solitude with his real guru, nature—and his teaching often emphasizes contact with nature as a resource for awakening.

Returning to Europe in 1995, he cofounded with his wife, Gail, the Tapovan Dharma Community in the French Pyrenees, where they raised their two children. As the number of visitors increased, they relocated in 2005 to Moulin de Chaves, a former Zen monastery in the Dordogne, southwest France.

Martin has taught retreats and guided students worldwide for over twenty years, drawing on his training in Buddhist Theravada practices, nondual teachings, and the Diamond Approach, with an emphasis on integrating spiritual depth of understanding into everyday breadth of experience.

Martin's teaching encourages and inspires a spiritual practice that both integrates meditation and daily activity and brings awakening to our true nature into the heart of our personal lives.

What to Read Next
from Wisdom Publications

A Heart Full of Peace
Joseph Goldstein

"In this short but substantive volume, Joseph Goldstein, who lectures and leads retreats around the world, presents his thoughts on the practice of compassion, love, kindness, restraint, a skillful mind, and a peaceful heart as an antidote to the materialism of our age."
—*Spirituality & Practice*

Awakening Together
The Spiritual Practice of Inclusivity and Community
Larry Yang
Forewords by Jan Willis and Sylvia Boorstein

"I don't see how *Awakening Together: The Spiritual Practice of Inclusivity and Community* could be better. It is so wise, thoughtful, and dedicated to our healthful growth, ease, and enlightenment through the Dharma that I know I will be reading it for years to come. Larry Yang seems to have thought of everything we will need as we venture bravely forward—through racism, prejudice, ignorance, and poor home training—into the free spiritual beings we were meant to be. Together."—Alice Walker, author of *The Color Purple*

The Way of Tenderness
Awakening through Race, Sexuality, and Gender
Zenju Earthlyn Manuel

"Manuel's teaching is a thought-provoking, much-needed addition to contemporary Buddhist literature."—*Publishers Weekly*

Mindfulness Yoga
The Awakened Union of Breath, Body, and Mind
Frank Jude Boccio

Editor's Choice—*Yoga Journal*

The Magnanimous Heart
Compassion and Love, Loss and Grief, Joy and Liberation
Narayan Helen Liebenson

The magnanimous heart is a heart of balance and buoyancy, of generosity and inclusivity. It allows us to approach each moment exactly as it is, in a fresh and alive way free from agendas and shoulds, receiving all that arises. It has the capacity to hold anything and everything, transforming even vulnerability and grief into workable assets.

Wholehearted
Slow Down, Help Out, Wake Up
Koshin Paley Ellison

"Intimacy is based on the willingness to open ourselves to many others, to family, friends, and even strangers, forming genuine and deep bonds based on common humanity. Koshin Paley Ellison's teachings share the way forward into a path of connection, compassion, and intimacy."—His Holiness the Dalai Lama

About Wisdom Publications

Wisdom Publications is the leading publisher of classic and contemporary Buddhist books and practical works on mindfulness. To learn more about us or to explore our other books, please visit our website at wisdomexperience.org or contact us at the address below.

Wisdom Publications
199 Elm Street
Somerville, MA 02144 USA

We are a 501(c)(3) organization, and donations in support of our mission are tax deductible.

Wisdom Publications is affiliated with the Foundation for the Preservation of the Mahayana Tradition (FPMT).